The Great
Marcus
Garvey

Liz Mackie

 A Hansib Educational Book

Marcus Garvey

"Becoming naturally restless for the opportunity of doing something for the advancement of my race, I was determined that the black man would not continue to be kicked about by all the other races and nations of the world...I saw before me then, even as I do now, a new world of black men, not peons, serfs, dogs and slaves, but a nation of sturdy men making their impress upon civilization and causing a new light to dawn on the human race."

Marcus Mosiah Garvey

Table of Contents

PART II   ARTICLES AND SPEECHES BY MARCUS GARVEY

First published in 1987 by Hansib Publishing Limited

Reprinted in 1997 by Hansib Caribbean
PO Box 2773, St John's, Antigua, WI

Distributed in the United Kingdom by Readers Book Club (Books Direct),
Tower House, 141-149 Fonthill Road, London N4 3HF
Fax: 0171-263 9656
Printed in the United Kingdom by The Bracken Press, Hatfield.

British Library Cataloguing in Publication Data.
A catalogue record for this book is available from the British Library

ISBN 1-870518-50-0

Biographical Details

1887	August 17, Marcus Garvey born, St Ann's Bay, Jamaica.
1907	Print Workers Strike.
1912-13	Garvey visits London.
1914	U.N.I.A. founded in Jamaica.
1916	March 23, Garvey arrives in the United States.
1918	*Negro World* established.
1919	Black Star Line established. Negro Factories Corporation established. December, Garvey marries Amy Ashwood.
1920	First U.N.I.A. convention, New York.
1921	Second U.N.I.A. convention, New York.
1922	July, Garvey marries Amy Jacques. August, Third U.N.I.A. convention, New York.
1923	May, Trial of Black Star Line directors begins.
1924	Fourth U.N.I.A. convention, New York. Negro Political Union formed.
1925	February, Garvey imprisoned in Atlanta.
1926	Fifth U.N.I.A. convention, Detroit.
1927	Garvey released and deported.

December 10, Garvey arrives in Kingston, Jamaica.

1928   April-September, Speaking tour of Europe.

1929   Sixth U.N.I.A. convention, Kingston.

People's Political Party founded.

September, Garvey convicted of contempt and imprisoned.

1930   Garvey elected to Kingston and St Andrew Corporation Council.

Jamaican Workers and Labourers Association founded.

September 17, Marcus Garvey Jnr born.

1933   August 16, Julius Garvey born.

1934 Seventh U.N.I.A. convention, Kingston.

1935   Garvey moves to London.

1938   Eighth U.N.I.A. convention, Toronto.

1940   June, Marcus Garvey dies, West Kensington, London.

Introduction

What you do today that is worthwhile, inspires others to act at
some future time.

[*Marcus Garvey*[1]]

There is a tide in the affairs of men.
Which, taken at the flood, leads on to fortune.

[*William Shakespeare*[2]]

The story of Marcus Garvey is that of a man who launched an idea
on the tide and created a flood in the world wide development of
black political consciousness. As the leader of America's first mass
political movement of black people, Garvey's achievements were
both enormous in their scale and long lasting in their effects. Garvey
changed the way that black Americans saw themselves. He taught
them that Africa was their spiritual home, at a time when most
thought their homelands were in the slave plantations; that Africa
was theirs to reclaim by right, while Europe's stranglehold on the
continent looked unassailable; that blackness was beautiful, when a
black skin was still a mark of servitude and a burden of shame. His
ideas spread to Europe, Africa and the Caribbean – to every place
where black people lived under the imperialist system of white rule;
and they too responded in their thousands to Garvey's call for a
'universal confraternity of the race'. Garvey's was the first and, as
yet, only internationalist, black mass movement.

There are few figures of the twentieth century who can be said to
have envisaged so much, completed so little, and inspired so many
as Garvey. Neither are there many people who have been found so
controversial. Since the 1960s, when the legacy of Garveyism
exploded on the world in the shape of Black Power and African
nationalism, Garvey has been subject to posthumous commenda-
tions and condemnations, similar to the mixture of admiration and
abuse he found in his lifetime. In some ways, Garvey was ahead of
his time – the actions of the 1960s were those he had been inciting

some forty years earlier. But essentially, his political views were a product of, and contribution to the 1920s; a decade which Garvey helped to make an unparallelled era of black achievement.

Most of Garvey's immediate ambitions came to nothing; he never did colonize Africa with Afro-Americans, nor did he create a class of black capitalists in America. He has therefore been labelled a failure by those who measure success in terms of tangible achievement or concrete change. There is no way to statistically monitor the impact of inspiration on peoples' lives. Garvey did not liberate Africa from colonialism, but he inspired Kenyatta, Nkrumah and others who did. Neither did he lead a black pressure group to make Civil Rights legal in the United States, but Martin Luther King recognized that the millions behind him would not be there but for the sense of "somebodiness" which Garvey had instilled in them. Other of Garvey's dreams have become realities; black pride and black solidarity meant little to few before Garvey turned them into a way of life.

Garvey's influence as a legacy to modern black politics is an accomplishment which overshadows but should not belittle his success in organizing a black political movement in his own lifetime. The Universal Negro Improvement Association (UNIA) was the biggest black organization the world had ever seen. It mobilized black activism across the globe, and provided a base from which other important political groups subsequently grew. The scale of Garvey's movement (with a reputed six million participants) is even more impressive when the factors mitigating against black organi- zation are considered. UNIA divisions were subject to scrutiny and harrassment by the imperialist powers in Africa and the Caribbean. In America, Garvey and his followers were persecuted by the Ku Klux Klan on the one side and the US Bureau of Investigation (forerunner of the F.B.I.) on the other. Many black Americans were hostile to Garvey's UNIA, some through political disagreement, and others through fear and ignorance. The latter was a common reaction to the innovation of Garveyism. The following, fictional, portrayal of Harlem, circa 1925, encapsulates those feelings;

"We shall be free" Our handsome leader promised.
"Our honourable Marcus Garvey shall be free..."
"Free! Free! Free!" the crowd chanted.
"We shall make good our vow. And we shall sail from these shores, back to the motherland, Africa! Africa! For we are Africans! "Africa for we Africans!" the crowd cheered. But they had lost me. Africa what damn Africa? Here I had just got to New York and loved it and these folks talking about leaving? I looked around at the hot faces, the thrown-back heads, the mouths tight and

determined. I had come to find Westindians, and instead found a bunch of Africans.

[Guy, pp40-41]

Black people in the Westindies and America were reared on a diet of white education, white politics, and inevitably adopted white ideas about African barbarism and backwardness. Small wonder that one of Garvey's greatest battles was against black peoples' refusal to see any commonality between themselves and those in Africa. "If Mr Garvey wanted to go to Africa" wrote a well-educated and prominent Jamaican citizen in 1930,

...let him go there by all means, but it is an insult to every Jamaican to tell him that his aim in life is to go back to African savagery.

[in Lewis, p.234]

In the face of such adversity, even his fiercest critics agree that Garvey stirred black Americans into unprecedented political action.

Garvey's own life was a mixture of triumph and tragedy. He grew up in a large family, of which only one sister was still alive by the time he reached his twenties. As a boy, Garvey did outstandingly well at school – where he also gained the unendearing nickname of 'Ugly Mug'. His first marriage to Amy Ashwood (a founder member of the UNIA), was a disaster which ended in separation after only three months. A childhood friend of Amy Ashwood went to New York at her invitation and became Garvey's second wife. Aside from Amy Jacques Garvey, Garvey appears to have been devoid of close friends or long term political allies. His uncompromising political stand alienated him from many one time associates with more pragmatic approaches, while his dedication to the UNIA left little time for personal relationships. Indeed, his marriage to Amy Jacques was politically rather than personally motivated, by her account:

He must have someone who had the right to be his personal representative – to act on his behalf and on his instructions...
He must get a wife...There were other eligibles among the membership but they lacked the sum total of qualities of what he wanted for a wife now – a stand-in, in an emergency. Again he turned to me, and very adroitly put the onus on me, stating that it was in my power to help the organization in this crisis. He had already obtained a divorce, so we were married...

[Jacques Garvey, a pp 88-89]

Although millions had followed him and thousands still idolized him, Garvey died alone, worn out and discredited at the age of 53.

He had not seen his wife or sons – aged six and nine – for over a year. But despite his ignominious end, it is probable that Garvey died knowing that the world would one day pay its tributes to him. He maintained a vision of himself as a world leader long after his movement had collapsed and its former glory was just a hazy memory to most. "Men who are in earnest are not afraid of the consequences" Garvey had once said, and few were as earnest as he. If a lonely death was the price of it, then Garvey must willingly have paid.

The opening words of Amy Jacques Garvey's biography of Marcus read:

> From early history to the present we learn of men and women who have emerged from their enviroment [sic] and so far out-distanced their contemporaries in thought and action, that in their day they were apt to be called "mad, dangerous or fools". Long after their death, when the truths they espoused or the experiments they conducted are validated, or the dangers which they pointed out came to pass, then they who have been convinced by experience are prone to admit that the visionary was right, and must have been inspired to be so persevering.
>
> [Jacques Garvey a p 1]

Clearly, Marcus Garvey was such a person.

PART I

Marcus Garvey in Perspective

Jamaica:
The Early Years

For over three hundred years the white man has been our
oppressor, and he naturally is not going to liberate us to the
higher freedom – the truer liberty – the truer Democracy. We
have to liberate ourselves.

(Marcus Garvey[3])

The tradition of black people's resistance to white oppression is as
old as the oppression itself. Throughout their centuries of enslavement black people fought – sometimes as individuals, sometimes
collectively – against the petty tyrannies and day to day brutalities
of the system. Some of those people are remembered for their heroic
defiance of the regime of exploitation – the Maroons, for instance –
but most of those who protested and died for their liberty have been
condemned to anonymity – the unsung heroes and heroines of
enslavement.

    After the British abolished slavery, leaving the white elite
hierarchy of colonial rule intact and in place, black people's
resistance to their materially unaltered conditions continued and
even flourished, as Emancipation proved itself a technical rather
than practical reality. Blacks stopped simply protesting and started
demanding; political rights, economic opportunity and social equality. Such were the demands voiced by Paul Bogle for the peasants
who confronted the might of white colonialism in the Morant Bay
Rebellion of 1865. The violent suppression of the rebellion under
Governor Eyre sparked off a significant controversy in Britain, but
its immediate effects were most strongly felt by the Jamaican
people. The incitement towards resistance had taken a crushing
blow and left the overwhelming majority of blacks hesitant to
proclaim their grievances against the colonizing authorities.

The latter decades of the nineteenth century marked the hightide of British imperialism. By the end of the century, Britain was reaping the benefits of Europe's partitioning of Africa, and had replaced the Caribbean with the Indian sub-continent as the new jewel in the Empire's crown. Against the increasing strength of Britain's colonial hold, opposition from Jamaica's disenfranchised and unarmed blacks became only a remote possibility.

Perhaps the greatest weapon Britain deployed in the continuing subjugation of colonial peoples was education. The colonial education system was a limited one but after centuries in which knowledge and learning had been denied to slaves, it was much sought after. It was through education, however that the most effective importation of Britain's imperialist ideology and colonial ethos took place. Generations of young Jamaicans learned to admire Britain's entrepreneurial world management, to depise Africa as a savage and backward continent, and to pray for their imperial figurehead – Queen Victoria. The legacy of colonial schooling was the saturation of British values and ideals, which demanded the corresponding negation of black history, black achievement, and black self-respect. Thousands of replicated Englishmen were created in this way; schooled to perpetuate the rationales for Britain's on-going hegemony in the Caribbean, in terms of a profound admiration for the English – their culture and their colour – which lasted long into the twentieth century. A man recalls his schooldays in colonial St Vincent:

> ...we prayed for Sir Francis Drake and Sir Walter Raleigh;...and we wore, uncomplainingly, green woolen blazers and grey flannel trousers to school, not because they were comfortable (the wool itched and stank in the tropical heat) but because on some decaying street in Liverpool as well as at a posh public school a British teenager wore the same get up.
>
> (in Lowenthal p268)

The veneration of English life (mirrored throughout the Caribbean in the appraisal of European 'parentlands') and the acceptance of its propogation in the tropics, proved Britain's greatest insurance against the possibility of dissent and opposition to colonial rule.

In the transition from the brutal exploitation of slavery to the more subtle but no less exploitative domination by colonialism, the black impetus towards resistance saw one of its final expressions in the Morant Bay Rebellion before its near complete suppression under the weight of imperial ideology – Britain's most successful nineteenth century import to the colonies.

Yet the dissenting voices were never completely silenced. Margi-

nalized, not only in their opposition to the white power elite but to
the mainstream of black society now entrenched in the mores of its
colonizers, radical and militant blacks continued to speak out
against the rule of oppression. Robert Love and Alexander Bedward
found outlets for their anti-colonial beliefs in militant journalism
and religious fervour respectively. Bedward's preaching had nationalist implications which attracted a sizeable following, as well as
concerned attention from the authorities, "Let them remember the
Morant War" he warned in a sermon [in Lewis], p35] – belieing the
notion that the Rebellion's crushing defeat had totally obliterated
the spirit of resistance. A worrying insurrectionist to the British,
Bedward was committed to a mental asylum in 1921. Dr Robert
Love published many fierce critiques of colonial rule in the *Jamaica
Advocate* (1894-1905). In 1904 he wrote:

> ...Englishmen will wake up some day to find they are making a great
> mistake...The subject races will not always be governed by that spirit. They were
> not always thus governed. The Indian will someday repel the assumption, the
> African will do the same thing, the Egyptian and Burmese etc., will vindicate
> their individuality and will prove that temporary dominance is not evidence of
> constitutional superiority.
>
> [in Lewis p33]

Coming at a time when the British pursuit for proof of their
'constitutional superiority' had already become a national obsession,
Love's statements were wholly seditious. It was probably his lack of
a popular following (for the authorities to translate as "stirring up
the natives") which saved Love from a similar fate to Bedward's.
Instead he lived to write into old age on the themes of anti-colonial
struggle, Pan-African organization and black class consciousness,
and to become an early and lasting influence on Marcus Garvey.

Marcus Garvey was born 22 years after and 100 or so miles away
from the historic events at Morant Bay. He was the result of his
father's third marriage – to Sarah Jane Richards – and one of only
two surviving children of the eleven fathered by Marcus Garvey Snr.
Marcus and Sarah Garvey would have been relatively affluent were
it not for a series of inept court actions brought by Marcus Snr
against his neighbours, resulting in the loss of their land plots to
pay the court costs and leaving the family with just its house.
Through a combination of formal schooling and private tuition,
Garvey Jnr received a more thorough education than was characteristic for black, working class children at that time. Even so, and to
Garvey's lasting bitterness, his school days were over at the age of
fourteen, when he became apprenticed to his godfather to learn

printing for three years, before moving to Kingston to take up his trade. In November 1908, the Printer's Union went on strike for higher wages and an eight hour working day. Garvey, now working in the print section of a pharmaceutical firm joined the strikers despite his prestigious position as a master printer and foreman. Amid allegations of treachery (the union treasurer apparently absconded with the strike fund), the management broke the strike with imported labour, reinstated most of the workers, but black-listed Garvey as the only foreman who had joined the strike. This early committment to trade unionism was to remain an important, though secondary feature of Garvey's political outlook.

Through 1910 and 1911, Garvey travelled through Central and South America, picking up casual work on the plantations. Here, the early learnt printing skills which were to become so essential to Garvey's political activism were put to such use. Garvey's visits to Costa Rica and Panama were marked by his publication of newspapers – *La Nacionale* and *la Prensa* – to express the views of the exploited migrant workers there. On his return to Jamaica, Garvey headed a delegation to put the case of Westindian migrant workers to the governor of Jamaica. This was characteristic of Garvey's political stance at the time, in which he regarded reform within the system as the only effective means of social change.

A visit to England (after some difficulty in securing the money for his fare) in 1912 was a decisive experience for Garvey in many ways. As a further dimension to his travel observations, Garvey's view of the universal nature of black people's oppression was consolidated by the realization that racism was not unique to the colonies but endemic in European society as well.

> I started to take an interest in the politics of my country, and then I saw the injustice done to my race because it was black, and I became dissatisfied on that account. I went travelling to South and Central America and parts of the Westindies to find out if it was so elsewhere, and I found the same situation. I set sail for Europe to find out if it was different there, and again I found the same stumbling block – "You are black".
>
> [Garvey b p126]

As an external student at Birkbeck College, London, where he attended Law classes, Garvey found a degree of satisfaction in the pursuit of education which meant so much to him. And with his contact with African nationalists in London, came Garvey's first understanding of the commonality of black struggles across the world. It was in England that the seeds of Garvey's vision of international black liberation were sown; that his enlightenment to his role of 'race leader' occurred;

I asked; "Where is the black man's Government?""Where is his King and his kingdom?""Where is his President, his country, and his ambassador, his army, his navy, his men of big affairs?" I could not find them, and then I declared, "I will help to make them."

[Garvey b p127]

Within five days of his return to Jamaica in 1914, Marcus Garvey formed the Universal Negro Improvement Association and African Communities (Imperial) League.

The Universal Negro Improvement Associations (UNIA) original programme was based on the following goals:

GENERAL OBJECTS

To establish a Universal Confraternity among the race.
To promote the spirit of race, pride and love.
To reclaim the fallen of the race.
To administer to and assist the needy.
To assist in civilizing the backward tribes of Africa.
To strengthen the Imperialism of independent African states.[4]
To establish Commissionaries or Agencies in the principal countries of the world for the protection of all Negroes, irrespective of nationality.
To promote a conscientious Christian worship among the native tribes of Africa.
To establish Universities, Colleges and Secondary Schools for the further education and culture of the boys and girls of the race.
To conduct a worldwide commercial and industrial intercourse.

LOCAL (JAMAICA) OBJECTS

To establish educational and industrial colleges for the further education and culture of our boys and girls.
To reclaim the fallen and degraded (especially the criminal class) and help them to a state of good citizenship
To administer to and assist the needy.
To promote a better taste for commerce and industry.
To promote a universal confraternity and strengthen the bonds of brotherhood and unity among the races.
To help generally in the development of the country.

[in Hill a p60]

In its early outlook the UNIA's political commitment was to the educational reformist approach epitomised by the black American leader Booker T Washington. The first local object was a move to found a replica of Washington's Tuskegee Institute in Jamaica, with the aim of teaching young blacks vocational skills as a means of effecting gradual social change. Its original aims also reflect the UNIA's attitude towards Africa, which was to remain ambiguous throughout the organization's existence. To bring the importance of

Africa to the black people of the diaspora was implicit in the programme's specific references to Africa. But so too was a paternalistic attitude towards the 'backward tribes', which demonstrates the colonial saturation of imperialist ideology, and which later found expression in Garvey's plans to 'colonize' Africa with American blacks. The UNIA's objects became far more elaborate as the movement grew, and changed in fundamental ways; but the early committment to simultaneous local and international perspectives remained integral.

For two years Garvey fought to establish his Association; a struggle not so much against the colonial government as against the black bourgeoisie and intelligentsia of the island. The 'coloured gentry', as Garvey called them, enjoyed a certain economic standing and social status within Jamaican society, which differentiated them from the black working class. Nobody amongst the upwardly mobile coloureds took kindly to Garvey's suggestion that coloureds and blacks were Negroes alike, and should organise on that basis. Decades had gone into carving out a small niche of coloured privilege, and more than Garvey's campaigning would be needed to alter that. Given the accommodating attitude towards the colonial authorities of the UNIA's programme at this stage, it is unsurprising that Garvey perceived the white ruling class as more sympathetic to his organization than the coloured middle classes.

They opposed me at every step, but I had a large number of white friends who encouraged and helped me. Notable among them were the then Governor of then Colony, the Colonial Secretary and several other prominent men. But they were afraid of offending the "coloured gentry" that passed for white.

[Garvey b p127]

Consequently, the UNIA received no support from Jamaica's more affluent citizens, and Garvey was without the backing he needed to promote his organization. This experience was at the root of Garvey's dislike of the 'black-whites' of Jamaica; the coloureds who, as Garvey saw it, tried to be white. It was inevitable that he should meet this stumbling block. In a society where class and colour were inextricably linked in a hierarchy descending from the white elite to the black poor, a light skin was a social passport to the middle ground. Garvey's call for a 'universal confraternity among the race' consciously appealed for an end to the divisive distinctions between black and brown, light and dark, Negro and Mulatto. But to those who benefitted from the system, the idea of 'universal negritude' was seen quite literally as a move to denigrate them. Much of Garvey's later hostility towards light skinned blacks must be understood as the reaction of a man socialized within the colour-coded stratification of the colonial Caribbean. One of his major political mis-judgements was to project the Jamaican colour hierarchy onto the American scene, and thus became embroiled in attacks on Harlem's 'coloured gentry' which were meaningless to most Americans; black was black, white was white, and no middle status had ever evolved there.

Faced with coloured hostility and black indifference to his liberationist race programme, Garvey continued undaunted in his proposals to establish a Tuskagee-style college in Jamaica. Despite Booker T Washington's death in 1915, Garvey went ahead with a planned visit to the Tuskagee Institute to learn more about his educational ideal and to elicit American financial support for the UNIA. With the possible exception of Garvey himself, no one recognized the Jamaican who arrived in the United States in March 1916, as the man (whose short visit stretched to eleven years) set to become the leader of the biggest Afro-American movement ever seen.

Background and Conditions in the United States

The world does not count races and nations that have nothing.
Point me a weak nation and I will show you a people
oppressed, abused, taken advantage of by others.
Show me a weak race and I will show you a people reduced
to serfdom, peonage and slavery.
Show me a well organized nation, and I will show you a
people and a nation respected by the world.

[Marcus Garvey[5]]

Marcus Garvey's inauspicious arrival in the United States came at a precipitous point in black American history. The convergence of three major factors – the war-time economy, the post-war anti-colonial backlash, the growing Pan-African movement – created a widespread Afro-American desire for social change during the early twentieth century, culminating in the 1920s with an explosion of black expression in politics and culture. For all his remarkable characteristics, Garvey's immense popularity was essentially a sign of the times. He focused and vocalised the massive discontent of the black population. The inspiration for, and cohesion of his mass following were uniquely the result of Garvey's skills as a leader and spokesman; but to explain the sheer scale of his movement we must look towards historical circumstance.

If the nineteenth century was 'probably the most humiliating century in the history of the Negro race' [Lynch p1], then the tables turned with the dawning of the twentieth century. In 1900, the first Pan-African Conference was convened in London. Thirty-seven delegates from around the world met to discuss the racist injustices imposed by colonial political rule and imperialist economic exploitation of black people. The conference's resolutions reflected the emergent consciousness of black solidarity and the stirrings of organized anti-colonialism;

1. To secure to Africans throughout the world true civil and political rights.
2. To meliorate the conditions of our brothers on the continent of Africa, America and other parts of the world.
3. To promote efforts to secure effective legislation and encourage our people in educational, industrial and commercial enterprise.
4. To foster the production of writing and statistics relating to our people everywhere.
5. To raise funds for these purposes.

[in Fryer pp284-5]

The Pan-African Movement remained small – its intellectual leanings proved fatally self-restricting – but was nonetheless important in the formation of ideas about black self-identity and the conception of Africa as the black homeland. Many of the early Pan-Africanists were influential in the development of later black political movements; W.E.B. Du Bois, present at the 1900 Conference, went on to lead the National Association for the Advancement of Colored People (NAACP) in America, and Duse Mohamed Ali was an inspiration to Garvey during the latter's visit to England in 1912.

While the Pan-Africanists continued to work and meet through the early twentieth century, other international events created a tide of change in the aspirations of black people which brought them instinctively, if not intellectually closer to the Pan-African ideals. The First World War altered the lives of millions of people far removed from the European battlefields. The United States felt the effects of the war long before entering as an 'associated power' in April, 1917. Chiefly, war-time conscription dried up the sources of European immigrant labour and indigenous workers, which were essential to Northern American industry. In a bid to secure alternative means of cheap labour, Northern industrialists turned to the Southern states and successfully campaigned for workers amongst the black sharecroppers. Between 1916 and 1918 up to half a million black people migrated from South to North. But the promises of full employment and freedom from Southern racist bigotry were short lived. With the war's end, thousands of blacks were sacked from factory jobs to make way for the returning, demobilized whites. And even for those blacks still in work, the illusion of Northern equality was rapidly fading.

Their initial feeling of delight at the comparative equality of treatment in the North rapidly gave way to a wave of discouragement as it became apparent that even in the fabled North Negroes were still only second class citizens, herded into black ghettoes, the last to be hired and the first to be fired.

[Cronon p27]

In the war's aftermath, black disillusionment grew as the American government failed to fulfil its wartime promises to the nation. Nearly 400,000 blacks had served in the United States armed forces, and millions more had supported the Wilson government's war-effort, presented as an appeal for the preservation of democracy. Afro-Americans held high hopes that some of the democratic freedom they fought to save would come their way after the war. By the summer of 1919 it was clear that they had been wrong.

While black and whites competed for jobs in Northern cities, the Ku Klux Klan was reborn in the South, in a reaction against the internationalistic spirit of the war years. By the early 1920s the Klan was boasting a membership of four million – an undoubtedly exaggerated figure but still a frightening reflection of its widespread white support. Aggravated by the Ku Klux Klan, racial tensions flared across the United States. In 1919, 76 blacks were lynched (the highest number in over a decade), and reports that some of these were uniformed soldiers returning from Europe outraged the black population. But black people's days as the exclusive victims of racial violence were over. When the sporadic conflicts throughout the year erupted into full scale rioting during the summer months, blacks armed themselves and fought back against the white mobs. Across America, discontent and resentment were expressed in violent confrontation between blacks and whites.

The riots in Chicago, Tulsa, Washington D.C., Charleston and a dozen or so more U.S. cities were part of a pattern of aggression and resistance playing out in violent clashes around the world. 1919 was the year in which the African National Congress started a resistance campaign against South Africa's pass laws. In India, General Dyer led the massacre at Amritsar – slaughtering the participants of a demonstration against colonial rule. Black workers in Sierra Leone, Trinidad, Panama and Costa Rica went on strike against racist employment practices. In England, rioting broke out in Liverpool and Cardiff when gangs of white men roamed the streets attacking demobilized colonial soldiers stranded in the cities. Disturbances were reported in Jamaica as a reaction to the Liverpool incidents. The British were seriously concerned about the level of anti-colonial agitation which was sweeping the Empire. A report of the Versailles conference in 1919 from an American

intelligence agent to the Washington State Department, contained
the following observations;

> [A British delegate] told me of the strikes and political disturbances in Sierra
> Leone, Jamaica and other British colonies where Blacks far outnumber Whites.
> The British seem very apprehensive of a united movement on the part of the
> coloured race and are making special enquiries into the racial cohesion or unity
> among the coloured races generally.
>
> [in May and Cohen p124]

Although mass organization of blacks was still embryonic in 1919,
the British had clearly recognised the black solidarity developing
synchronically around the world. Their apprehension was certainly
called for; Britain's days of divide and rule were numbered.

The blacks who armed themselves and fought back against their
centuries-long oppression by white society, were the 'New Negroes'
of Garvey's speeches. "the Uncle Tom nigger has got to go" warned a
delegate to the 1920 UNIA convention, "and his place must be taken
by the new leader of the Negro race" [in Cronon]. The 'New Negro'
was to 'Uncle Tom' what Garvey was to become to Booker T
Washington; militant and uncompromising as against passive and
accommodating; demanding rights not asking for reforms.the
UNIA, NAACP, and other black organizations shaped the 'New
Negroes' into people committed to social change through the power
of mass political action. But the new spirit of black confidence was a
forerunner to, rather than a product of Garveyism. While Garvey
was still finding his way around New York, inspired blacks were
laying the foundations for movements that channelled the bitter
disillusionment of the post-war years into the explosion of cultural
and political creativity which burst upon America in the 1920s.

Garvey's UNIA took up the threads of existing Pan-Africanist
ideas, tapped the current of resentment in the black population and
became the major political expression of black discontent. Du Bois'
NAACP similarly captured the mood of an embittered black
community ready to turn fading hopes into enthusiastic activism.
The same force pioneered a new and exciting era of black cultural
achievement; coalescing in the now legendary Harlem Renaissance.
Black artists, writers and musicians turned Harlem into the
cultural capital of the black world. Some achieved lasting fame,
others dropped rapidly back to obscurity, but all were part of the
upsurge in black militancy; black and proud and fighting. Just a few
names from that decade of innovation read like a roll-call of
America's finest artists; Billie Holiday, Langston Hughes, Zora
Neale Hurston, Bessie Smith, Claude McKay, James Weldon

Johnson, Duke Ellington, Paul Robeson, Josephine Baker. Although less self-consciously 'political' than Garveyism, the Harlem Renaissance was nonetheless a profound political expression.

> Not everyone wrote [or danced, or sang] about "being black", but they were black and they were artists; that was – and is – a statement in itself.
>
> [Dennis and Willmarth p134]

Three distinct trends of black activism were thus born from the shattered dreams of the post-war years; the large-scale political involvement of the UNIA, the development of a radical black intelligentsia in the NAACP, the cultural expression of blackness in the Harlem Renaissance. The intellectual movement was in many ways a part of the cultural renaissance, and Garvey was largely isolated from and in conflict with Harlem's leading lights. But...

> ...the same forces that stimulated the Negro Renaissance helped to create an audience for Garveyism. Garvey's bombastic efforts to whip up an intense black nationalism were a logical counterpart to the more subtle but equally militant contemporary verse of such Negro poets as Claude McKay, Langston Hughes, and Countee Cullen.
>
> [Cronon p171]

The UNIA in the United States

The world ought to know that it could not keep 400,000,000 Negroes down forever.

[Marcus Garvey[6]]

Garvey's arrival in the United States swept away his political reformism. In the face of Southern segregation and the Northern colour bar, the overt and violent racism of the United States called for militant action rather than peaceful pleas for reform. "If Washington had lived he would have had to change his program" Garvey observed,

> No leader can successfully lead this race of ours without giving an interpretation of the awakened spirit of the New Negro, who does not seek industrial opportunity alone, but a political voice. The world is amazed at the desire of the New Negro, for with his strong voice he is demanding a place in the affairs of men.
>
> [Garvey b p56]

Garvey was quick to adapt his political ideas to his new environment, and launched his appeal for black solidarity from a soap-box in New York's Lenox Avenue. His gift for public speaking soon attracted excited attention and invitations from left-wing organisers to address their meetings. Fifteen months after arriving in America, Garvey had lectured in 'Boston, Washington, Philadelphia, Chicago, Milwaukee, St Louis, Detroit, Cincinnati, Indianapolis, Louisville, Nashville and other cities' [Vincent p100]. The UNIA chapter Garvey had established in Harlem, had about 1000 members by the end of 1917.

In 1918, Garvey started his most ambitious and successful publishing venture: The *Negro World*. The *Negro World* was published weekly from 1918 to 1933, and achieved the highest circulation of any black paper of that time (estimated at between 60,000 and 200,000 during its best years). Distributed in Africa and the Caribbean as well as America, the *Negro World* was crucial to the cohesion of Garvey's growing international movement. For this very reason, the paper was banned in several countries (its possession carried the death penalty in French colonial Dahomey), by imperialist governments worried at the effects of its insurrection-ism on an already troublesome 'native problem'. A report by the British Cabinet Office in November 1919 indicates the role the *Negro World* was playing in stirring anti-colonial feelings;

> Reports from a reliable source indicate that the Negro agitation is beginning to assume international proportions. Large quantities of propoganda [sic] litera-ture, calculated to incite racial ill-feeling, have been shipped from the United States to Africa and the Westindies. Marcus Garvey's *Negro World,* which is published in New York, already has a wide circulation among the Negroes in the Westindies and Africa, and its teaching has already caused trouble in the zone of the Panama Canal.
>
> [in Hill d p153]

The *Negro World* became the mouthpiece of Garveyism; charting the UNIA's progress around the world, disseminating the political principles of Garveyism, and printing frequent appeals for financial support. As editor of the *Negro World,* Garvey consistently refused to accept lucrative advertising for skin bleaching creams, hair straightening lotions, or anything else designed to 'whiten' black people. The paper's name was itself a political statement, as Garvey later explained;

> I started the "Negro World" to preserve the term Negro to the race as against the desperate desire of other newspapermen to substitute the term "coloured" for the race.
>
> [Garvey b p78]

In part Garvey was sniping at Du Bois, the NAACP and their journal *Crisis,* but overall the name 'Negro World' was part of Garvey's endeavour to appropriate 'Negro' as an honourable term for black people at a time when its corruption to 'nigger' was far more common, and 'coloured' was unacceptable to a Jamaican for its non-black connotations.

Through the *Negro World,* black Americans learned of Garvey's first, most adventurous and most disastrous black commercial enterprise. The Black Star Line (BSL) established in 1919, was the embodiment of the UNIA's belief that black people's success lay in their divorce from white capital and their organization of black

A Black Star Line stock certificate

The *Yarmouth,* the ill-fated first ship of the Black Star Line. In 1920 the *Yarmouth* carried teams of UNIA recruiters around the Caribbean

business and industry; an aspect of Booker T Washington's theories which continued to influence Garvey. By the same token, the UNIA founded the Negro Factories Corporation (NFC) in the same year. Among the business developed by the NFC were a chain of co-operative grocery shops, a restaurant, a steam laundry, a tailor and dressmaking shop, a milliners and a publishing house.

The *Negro World* advertised and promoted sales of BSL stock; the newly increased urban black population responded enthusiastically. Through 1919 and 1920, some three-quarters of a million dollars was collected for the shipping enterprise – much of it coming from ordinary and impoverished blacks inspired by the magnitude of Garvey's plans. A Bureau of Investigation informant reported in July, 1920;

> There seems to be an unlimited amount of money coming in from shares in the Black Star Line. I registered letters today for over four hundred thousand dollars, most of it from the Westindies and the central part of the United States. One old woman down in Virginia wrote she was old and poor but she was sending twenty-five dollars towards the "cause", because she wanted to go home to Africa.
>
> [in Hill d p424]

Returning people to Africa was not the avowed intention of the BSL. The SS *Yarmouth* (renamed Frederick Douglass) was intended to run the trade routes to the Caribbean, with the *Phyllis Wheatley* (which never materialised) trading between America and Africa. "Through the Black Star Line we will come into trade relations with our bretheren on the West Coast of Africa", explained Garvey in 1920 [in Cronon p77]. Along with *Yarmouth,* the BSL bought and launched SS *Shadyside* and SS *Kanawha* (renamed Antonio Maceo).

The climax of Garvey's American career came in 1920 with the UNIA's first convention. The International Convention of the Negro People of the World opened on August 1, 1920, with two thousand delegates from twenty-five countries in attendance. The inaugural parade through the streets of Harlem was a stunning exhibition of the UNIA's organizational achievements and thousands-strong membership. Marching behind the UNIA band were two hundred Black Cross Nurses, the Universal Africa Motor Corps, the Black Eagle Flying Corps, the African Legion, the UNIA choir and the juvenile auxiliary.

> This pageantry drew thousands of onlookers and constituted a bold symbolic demonstration that African people had to stand up and stake their own claims for dignity and self-determination.
>
> [Lewis p85]

On the night of August 1, 25,000 people packed into Madison Square Gardens to hear Garvey's opening address. To a five minute standing ovation from a crowd waving the newly adopted flags of red, black and green, Garvey delivered his legendary speech;

> We shall now organize the 400,000,000 Negroes of the world into a vast organization to plant the banner of freedom on the great continent of Africa...If Europe is for the Europeans, then Africa shall be for the black peoples of the world.
>
> [in Edwards p15]

Over the next three weeks the convention delegates were in conference, discussing the world situation of black people and endorsing strategies for change. The new colours of the movement were officially accepted; red for the blood shed in black struggle; black as a symbol of pride; green for the new life in Africa. Garvey was elected Supreme Potentate of the UNIA and Provisional President of the African Republic, and an entire administrative hierarchy was established with an annual salary of $12,000 awarded to top officials. On August 13, the convention adopted the

A mammoth parade through Harlem revealed to the world the strength of Garvey movements. The 1920 convention opened and closed with big parades which included marching groups of Black Cross nurses and the paramilitary African Legion

UNIA Convention parade, Harlem, August 1920

'Declaration of the Rights of the Negro People of the World' – the
UNIA's single most important statement of principles and intentions. A decision to campaign for the capitalization of the word
'Negro' was a small but significant achievement for the convention;
the New York State Board of Education ratified this proposal in
1929 as a direct result of UNIA pressure.

The 1920 convention was both a resounding success for the UNIA
and a triumph for the acceptance of African nationalism. Garvey's
tentative anti-colonialism had matured to a comprehensive nationalist philosophy embraced by the hundreds of thousands who
heard him expound it. "And in the making of Africa a big black
republic, what is the barrier?" Garvey asked the crowd in Carnegie
Hall at the convention's close,

> The barrier is the white man; and we say to the white man who now dominates
> Africa that it is to his interest to clear out of Africa now, because we are coming
> not as in the time of Father Abraham, 200,000 strong, but we are coming
> 400,000,000 strong, and we mean to retake every square inch of the 12,000,000
> square miles of African territory belonging to us by right Divine.
>
> [in Cronon p66]

The convention established Garvey as the leading political figure in
the black world; the UNIA membership swelled and millions more
blacks looked to Harlem, and Garvey for direction.

It is not known exactly how many people were directly involved in
Garvey's UNIA. The Association's own records were incomplete and
contemporary estimates varied enormously. The number of official
members in the United States was probably more than one million
over the years. But this figure underestimates the sphere of
Garvey's influence;

> In computing the membership of the organization, to say that it was about six
> million is no exaggeration; yet it can never be accurately arrived at, as there are
> divisions, branches and chapters of the UNIA, besides chapters of Garveyites
> under different names in fraternities, and "pockets" of Garveyism as a
> philosophy among study groups etc...
>
> The man, woman or child who has heard Garvey speak, or has read his
> writings becomes inspired, and if converted to Garveyism is a changed person in
> outlook; however, most of them will not give him credit for the change.
>
> [Jacques Garvey a pp264-5]

The UNIA had divisions throughout the world, with 120,000 paid up
members in the Caribbean and Latin America, and a further 30,000
in Africa. Due to the colonial suppression of political groups though,
many active Garveyites were obliged to keep their allegiance secret.

Where modern historians quibble about the size of Garvey's movement they do so in millions rather than thousands.

Garvey changed people's lives. he taught millions of Afro-Americans to be proud of their colour and strong in their blackness. And for thousands of his followers, these simple tenets of Garveyism became a way of life. A one time Garveyite recalled;

> 'Garvey children' were taught about Marcus Garvey, George Washington Carver, and about heroic black women like Harriet Tubman and Sojourner Truth. They had to learn one Garvey poem a week, read Harriet Beecher Stowe's *Uncle Tom's Cabin*, and were shown pictures and carvings of black angels and were given black dolls.
>
> [in Lewis p69]

Even in the Southern states, where the Ku Klux Klan resurged in a backlash against this new generation of 'uppity niggers', Garveyite households sprang up defiantly. In mid-western Nebraska, Malcolm X was born into a Garveyite family; he described his father as;

> A typical Garveyite, he was making his first step towards economic independence by building his own store. At the time we were the only Negroes in the block. Then two years later my father was found with his head bashed in and his body mangled under a street car.
>
> [in Essein-Udom p96]

Garveyism threatened the foundations of white supremacy, and worried racists, unable to attack the heart of the movement, intimidated and assaulted Garvey's more isolated followers.Their lives were often at risk, but still blacks across the United States stood up to be counted amongst those who rallied to Garvey's call for liberation.

"There has never been a Negro movement anywhere like the Garvey movement" wrote C.L.R. James, "and few movements in any country can be compared to it in growth and intensity" [James b p68]. Never before had anyone given black Americans so much to work towards and so many visions to fulfil. Garvey offered success (in the development of black business), hope (in the emancipation of Africa) and racial equality at the end of the road. The UNIA gave training (in military, nursing and engineering skills), education (in African and black American history) and displays of black pomp and circumstance such as America had never seen. From the men and women in Africa who translated the *Negro World's* message into the fight for nationalist freedom, to the boys and girls brought up with black dolls and black heroes, Garvey inspired change.

Garvey's support and popularity remained consistently high in the early and mid-1920s, but serious financial difficulties set in not long after the spectacular success of the first convention. After its impressive launch the BSL floundered in a sea of mis-management and commercial cons. The *Yarmouth* the BSL's flagship, first set sail late in 1919 under the command of Captain Joshua Cockbourne. Plagued with engine troubles and a riotously undisciplined crew, the ship was in operation for less than two years. Garvey fired Cockbourne for mismanagement after *Yarmouth's* second voyage and replaced him with a white Canadian captain for the third and final journey. The *Shadyside* was bought as an excursion boat, and made many trips up and down the Hudson during the 1920 convention. But after only five months, the BSL directors had no choice but to take the grossly inefficient *Shadyside* out of service. In that short space of time the ship had cost the company $11,000 in operating losses. Unusable and unsaleable, the *Shadyside* sank in the Hudson during the winter of 1921. The BSL bought its third and largest ship – the SS *Kanawha* – at the inflated price of $60,000, a payment it never managed to complete. The *Kanawha* lived up to the now established tradition of BSL disaster and blew out a boiler manhole on its maiden voyage, scalding a crew member to death. The boilers gave out again on the *Kanawha's* second attempted trip, and the ship had to be towed into a Virginian port for more repairs. After a few equally fraught voyages, the BSL abandoned the *Kanawha* in Antilla Harbour, Cuba, in 1921. Against operating costs of nearly $135,000, the *Kanawha* had brought in a mere $1,207 in operating income. In total, from the three quarters of a million dollars raised from the sale of BSL stock, the company's cash balance in May 1922 was just $31.12 [Cronon p113]

For a while Garvey was able to keep the BSL's failure a secret from his followers – of whom some 40,000 had invested money in the shipping line. The *Negro World* published optimistic proposals for a new ship – the *Phyllis Wheatley* – to the BSL fleet. Inevitably though, news of the company's collapse leaked out. To Garvey's critics, the event was a vindication of the "it will never work" line many of them had taken. Of the BSL investors, some felt outraged and betrayed, having backed Garvey's venture with their ill-affordable personal savings. Most, however, stood firmly behind their leader and 'unquestioningly accepted his bitter account of the dishonesty and treachery that had caused the downfall of the Black Star Line' [Cronon p108]. Treachery may have been an exaggeration of what went on, but the BSL directors were certainly taken for a ride in their naive entry into the worlds of high finance and commercial enterprises. All three of their ships were practically unseaworthy and sold to them at inflated prices by unscrupulous dealers. The few black 'experts' involved in the venture, including Cockbourne, proved themselves at best inept, at worst corrupt. The lesson of the BSL was perhaps the clearest illustration that some wisdom lay on Garvey's adaptation of Booker T Washington's theory of economic self-sufficiency as the only road to black achievement. Speculative as it may be, it is probable that the BSL would have fared better if black financial and technical expertise had been available. As it was, Garvey launched black business at the most ambitious end of the scale; and then found himself without a sound economic base or skilled workforce to prop up his project.

The downfall of the BSL landed four of its directors in court; Marcus Garvey (President), Eli Garcia (Secretary), George Tobias (Treasurer) and Orlando Thompson (Vice President). Garvey was right to view the trial as less an investigation of the BSL's alleged fraud than a bid to discredit the entire UNIA. May 1923 marked not just the trial's opening but the successful completion of a five year crusade by the U.S. Government to find grounds for removing Garvey from the political scene.

Garvey first came under official scrutiny as early as November 1918. In a report to the Bureau of Investigation on November 12, it was noted;

> His speech bordered closely on sedition in that he prophesied a revolution of the negroes of the United States unless their demands were granted. This man's nationality and antecedents will be closely investigated, and should it be found that he is not a citizen of the United States, an effort will be made to locate stenographic minutes of this meeting for the purpose of taking up questions of disposing of Garvey, who could easily become a menace in these times.
>
> [in Hill c p285]

Eventually, in 1927, Garvey's 'alien' nationality was used to deport him, but in the meantime the Bureau of Investigation mounted a surveillance operation of all Garvey's activities and UNIA meetings. Like the British, the American government could not fail to miss the post-war discontent amongst black populations. Nor did they hesitate in moving to rout out those they perceived as instigators of the unrest. With the full weight of the government's investigatory machinery bearing down on him, a state prosecution against Garvey was only a matter of time. J. Edgar Hoover was the architect of the Bureau's plans for Garvey. Almost everything was considered by the Bureau as possible grounds for Garvey's removal– sedition, incitement to riot, tax evasion – but it was Hoover who hit upon the winning idea. In October 1919, just months after the BSL was founded, Hoover made the following disclosure in a letter to a Garveyite informant;

> Unfortunately, however, [Garvey] has not as yet violated any federal law whereby he could be proceeded against on the grounds of being an undesirable alien, from the point of view of deportation. It occurs to me however, from the attached clipping, that there might be some proceeding against him for fraud in connection with his Black Star Line propoganda, and for this reason I am transmitting the communication to you for your appropriate mention.
>
> [in Hill d p72]

Early in 1922, Garvey and his three co-defendants were charged with using the mail to defraud.

Hoover and the Bureau of Investigation were not the only ones who wanted Garvey out of the way. The long running hostility between the UNIA and other black organizations (principally the NAACP) came to a head in 1922. During the third UNIA convention in Harlem, a number of his opponents held anti-Garvey meetings elsewhere in New York. Headed by Chandler Owen and A. Philip Randolph (editors of the radical *Messenger* journal), this group called themselves the Friends of Negro Freedom and their slogan was "Garvey must go". Speaking at public meetings, the Friends of Negro Freedom accused Garvey of complicity with the Ku Klux Klan, and denounced him as "egotistic, tyrannical, intolerant, cunning, shifty, smooth and suave, avaricious" [in Cronon p107]. Tensions ran high, and frequent scuffles broke out between anti-Garvey and Garvey supporters as each group turned out to heckle the others' meetings. Anti-Garveyites were further incensed when A. Philip Randolph received a packet through the post containing a human hand, purportedly from the Ku Klux Klan but, felt Randolph and others, more probably the work of a Garvey supporter.

On January 15, 1923, eight prominent black men and women (including Chandler Owen) signed an open letter to the Attorney General protesting at the eleven month delay in bringing Garvey's fraud case to trial. The "Committee of Eight" attacked Garvey as "an unscrupulous demagogue, who had ceaselessly and assiduously sought to spread among Negroes distrust and hatred of all white people" [in Garvey b p295]. Whether the letter influenced the Attorney General is unknown, but either way Garvey arrived in court four months later.

Garvey can be considered either boldly daring or uncommonly foolish (or both) in his decision to conduct his own defence. Drawing on the memory of his Birkbeck law lectures, Garvey, by all accounts, wore out the judge, lawyers, witnesses and jurors alike with his detours into long-winded examination of testifiers on obscure and irrelevant subjects. "Garvey, man of destiny, calmly awaits verdict" announced the *Negro World* while the jury deliberated. But to the disbelief of his supporters, Garvey was found guilty. The BSL co-defendants were acquitted, while Garvey received the maximum penalty for mail fraud; a $1,000 fine and five years imprisonment. The U.S. government had succeeded in pinning Garvey down under the thumb of the criminal justice system.

Out on bail and pending the result of his Appeal, Garvey's activism continued unabated.the UNIA's fourth convention, in 1924, inaugurated the Negro Political Union as a forum for the support of black political candidates. The Negro Political Union was the predecessor of the People's Political Party later established in Jamaica to greater effect.

Early in 1925, to his great astonishment, Garvey's appeal was dismissed. Even Garvey's critics saw the injustice in this and spoke out on his behalf. "He has been charged with dishonesty and graft" wrote W.E.B. Du Bois, "but he seems to me essentially an honest and sincere man with tremendous vision, great dynamic force, stubborn determination and unselfish desire to serve." [in Edwards p24]. Some white newspapers also backed the UNIA's claim of unfair sentencing. The New York *Evening Bulletin* conceded, "Garvey is a Negro, but even a Negro is entitled to have the truth told about him", while the Buffalo *Evening Times* asserted, "It is a grave question whether justice has been done in the case of Marcus Garvey..... If, for the sake of argument, every contention of the authorities be granted, there is still something that is not pleasant about this whole business." [ibid.]. Public opinion, however, made no difference to the Supreme Court's decision. In February 1925, Marcus Garvey was incarcerated in Atlanta prison.

That the UNIA remained largely intact and active during Garvey's absence was due both to the membership's support for its martyred leader and the unceasing efforts of Garvey's second wife. Under the provisional leadership of Amy Jacques Garvey, the UNIA continued its work; directed primarily at securing Garvey's release. By the end of 1925, Amy Jacques Garvey had edited and published a second, longer volume of her husband's writings and speeches (the first appeared in 1923). Together, these books – *Philosophy and Opinions of Marcus Garvey* – became the near definitive statement of Garvey's race philosophy. An emergency convention (the Fifth International Convention of the Negro Peoples of the World) was held in Detroit in March, 1926, to reaffirm allegiance to Garvey and

A UNIA protest parade, 1924

plan UNIA strategy for his release campaign. Early in 1927, the UNIA petitioned President Coolidge for clemency in Garvey's case. For all the UNIA's efforts, however, the organization began its inexorable decline during Garvey's imprisonment. Without Garvey's visible leadership, a move towards factionalism began amongst the UNIA divisions, and members started to drift away.

By December, the UNIA's efforts had paid off. Garvey's sentence was commuted and, after almost three years in prison, his immediate release was ordered. From the authorities' viewpoint, Garvey's continued imprisonment was unnecessary; they now had grounds for Garvey's removal from the United States albeit on a technical illegality.

> The government used a law which stipulated that an alien convicted of a felony within five years of his arrival in the United States could be deported. As Garvey's lawyers pointed out to no avail he had been in this country more than six years prior to his conviction.
>
> [Vincent p218]

A victim of the government's intentions to rid itself of America's most influential black radical, Garvey set sail for Jamaica in December 1927.

Marcus Garvey (third from left) on board the SS Saramacca before his deportation from New Orleans in 1927

Garvey's Later Years in Jamaica and England

There has never been a movement where the leader has not suffered for the Cause, and not received the ingratitude of the people. I, like the rest, am prepared for the consequence.
(Marcus Garvey)[7]

Marcus Garvey's reputation preceded him to Jamaica. "It is with profound regret that we view the arrival of Marcus Garvey back to Jamaica." wrote the island's *Daily Gleaner,* "And it is with even more profound regret that we picture any leader of thought and culture in the island associating himself with a welcome given him. But Kingston has reached such a level of degeneracy that there is no knowing what she will do..." [in Edwards p26]. Nevertheless, the paper was obliged to report that "Mr Garvey's arrival...was perhaps the most historic event that has taken place in the metropolis of the island...no denser crowd has ever been witnessed in Kingston." [in Lewis, p197]. Thousands of Jamaicans turned out to welcome home the man who had become their idol in his absence.

Garvey had planned to mark his return to Jamaica with an immediate tour of the Caribbean to widen the base of his support there. But no Central American government would permit visas for his entry, nor would the British allow him into any of their Westindian colonies. So instead, in the spring of 1928, Amy Jacques and Marcus Garvey journeyed to Europe. Little enthusiasm for Garveyism could be engendered amongst the British – "9800 Empty Seats" was the headline in the only paper which reported Garvey's speech in the Albert Hall on June 6. His reception was somewhat better in Paris and Geneva, but still a pale shadow of the magnificent crowds he had drawn a decade earlier.

Back in Jamaica, to where the colonial powers had effectively confined him, Garvey concentrated on building support for the local UNIA; within one month of his arrival, the Kingston branch was said to have doubled its membership. Yet, however keen was his Jamaican following, Garvey's foothold in international politics was slipping. His all-important political stronghold in the United States collapsed into factional warring which only Garvey's presence had prevented from happening sooner. And even if the American UNIA had remained intact, Garvey's physical separation from it destroyed the potential which had once existed in his mobilization of America's blacks. Jamaica had neither the worldwide signficance nor the mass population of the United States.

> ...his international impact was considerably weaker in Kingston than in Harlem...The most important reason was that in the 1920s Harlem was, in a sense, the cultural and political capital of the Black World, while Kingston was a relatively insignificant colonial city. It was in Harlem that Garveyism became important although Kingston had been the birthplace of the UNIA.
>
> [Lewis p184]

The world too had changed by the late 1920s. The optimism of the decade crashed with Wall Street and the onset of economic depression. As in other historical periods of severe financial hardship, mass political action gave way to the individual struggle for survival. Where the impetus for collective action could be found it was generating in a new and frightening direction. Mass movements across the globe developed to support supremacist and fascist leaders; Mussolini in Italy, the Ku Klux Klan in America, Moseley in Britain, Franco in Spain, Hitler in Germany. Garvey's vision no longer captured the mood of his time; and where his support remained strong, the money which people had once pledged to his plans was now needed to stave off hunger and starvation.

Not a man to be easily defeated, Garvey made 1929 an eventful year for his Jamaican activities. In July, a Chief Justice ruling on the case of G.D. Marke (a former UNIA official now sueing Garvey for his back pay), ordered the sale of all UNIA properties and assets in Jamaica. Everything was sold to pay Marke's salary, despite a pending appeal from the local UNIA. The appeal was successful, but came too late to salvage much from the financial damage already inflicted. The Isiah Morter case also came up in 1929; Morter's bequeathment of his fortune to the UNIA was contested by the U.S. UNIA against the Jamaican divisions. Again the ruling went against Garvey, with the judgement that Morter's money could not be left to the UNIA as this was for 'illegal purposes' [Jacques Garvey b p277]. The case cost the local UNIA thousands of pounds in costs and appeals, but the estate was eventually awarded to the American UNIA. From accounts of the trials proceedings it is clear that the Chief Justice's intent was to complete the task started by the United States of squeezing Garvey out of politics. Garvey's remarkable resiliance, however, complicated his silencing.

> Garvey and the movement were stripped financially, but their spirit was never broken; so they held the sixth international convention in Jamaica, and the delegates heralded to the world a defiance that whatever mortal men did to hamper the struggle, the spirit of Garveyism would prevail.
>
> [Jacques Garvey b p277]

The sixth convention consolidated the growing rift between Garvey and the leaders of the American UNIA. Garvey's insistence that the convention recognize Jamaica as the official headquarters of the movement led to a walkout by American delegates and resulted in the formal establishment of two seperate organizations; the U.S. leadership remained the UNIA (incorporated) 1918, and Garvey headed the UNIA (unincorporated) 1929.

In September, Garvey launched the People's Political Party (PPP) to contest seats in the forthcoming municipal elections and the general election of the following year. Garvey's entry into local politics was a recognition of the barriers facing him in the international sphere. Although local activity had always been theoretically central to Garvey's political programme, in practice his energy had been devoted far wider afield. However, the PPP was not concerned with purely local issues. The party's manifesto took a strong anti-imperialist stand; a radical step in Jamaican politics at that time. The manifesto also included promises for a minimum wage for workers, land reform, urban improvements and full employment. The government, however, did not need to look too closely at Garvey's campaign programme to find cause to obstruct it. The tenth point of the PPP's manifesto pledged;

> A law to impeach and imprison such judges who in defiance of British justice and constitutional rights will illicitly enter into agreements and arrangements with lawyers and other persons of influence to deprive other subjects in the realm of their rights in such courts of law over which they may preside, forcing the innocent parties to incur the additional costs of appeals, and other legal expenses which would not have been but for the injustice occasioned by the illicit arrangements of such judges with their friends.
>
> [in Lewis p210]

Garvey's own unhappy experiences in the Jamaican courts were responsible for his formulation of the tenth plank. The Morter and Marke cases had cost him dearly, but more significantly, had shown him the degree to which the courts could be manipulated by ruling class interests. After presenting the PPP manifesto at a public meeting, Garvey was charged and found guilty of contempt. He was sentenced to three months imprisonment.

Garvey won the municipal by-election for Kingston and St Andrew Corporation in October, whilst serving his prison sentence. Attempts made by Jamaica's ruling authorities to push Garvey off all political platforms was never so clearly seen as in the efforts made to keep him off his council seat. A stipulation that a councillor's non-attendance at three consecutive council meetings automatically made his seat vacant, was exploited to the full. Garvey wrote repeatedly from prison requesting leave of absence until the end of his sentence, but was each time rejected by council decision. The council gleefully declared Garvey's seat vacant on January 15 1930, despite the fact that Garvey had been out of prison for four weeks and had attended the council meeting on December 30. The council decision was made on legal advice, which can have done nothing to allay Garvey's hositility towards the legal and judicial system. Almost as a postscript to the entire affair, Garvey was re-elected to the council, unopposed, in February 1930.

His three months in prison lost Garvey not only his council seat but precious campaigning time for the January general election. The PPP backed twelve candidates, but the property requirements for election nominees narrowed the choice so considerably that few could be found who supported PPP policies. None of the candidates endorsed by the PPP defended the party's manifesto – one even went so far as to publish his own. At least two were managers in companies which Garvey had publicly denounced as exploiters of the working people. Clearly, most were aiming to cash in on the popularity of the UNIA and ran on the PPP slate for this, rather than for reasons of political affinity. The shortcomings of the candidates did not dampen Garvey's enthusiasm for the campaign. "The politics of Jamaica has received a wholesome stimulus from the advent of the People's Political Party" he proclaimed, adding that they "had already received results exceeding the expectations of many" [in Lewis p220].

But the PPP lost heavily in the elections; only three of the twelve candidates were elected to the Legislative Council. Garvey himself was defeated by 1677 votes to 915. The limited political franchise contributed significantly to the PPP's failure. Less than 8% of

Jamaicans were entitled to vote, and just one third of those actually did so [Hill p9]. Strangely, the PPP manifesto did not call for an extension of the franchise, although Garvey had previously argued that voting eligibility dependent on income (£52 per year) was too restrictive. The appeal of the PPP, with its emphasis on wage reforms and workers rights, was to precisely that section of the population ineligible to vote for it – the working class. The manifesto had anticipated another factor which Garvey subsequently analysed as partly responsible for the PPP's electoral downfall. Point nineteen called for;

> A law for the imprisonment of any person who by duress or undue influence would force another person to vote in any public election against his will, because of obligation or employment or otherwise.
>
> [Jacques Garvey b p278]

Garvey's run for office had been against George Seymour Seymour, a wealthy businessman who, incidentally, had blocked Garvey's appeals for leave of absence from the council. Seymour, Garvey alleged, bribed his way to the Legislative Council. "The people of my race," he raged, "were fed on rum, sugar and water and sandwiches, as a reward for their votes for Mr Seymour." [in Lewis p226]

Garvey's electoral defeat marked another stage in the decline of the UNIA as a major political force. The election results had frustrated Garvey's struggle to politicize the Jamaican blacks to the point where he denounced the community as "limited in intelligence and narrow in its intellectual concepts" [in Lewis 230]. Although addressed primarily to the black voters who had failed him, Garvey's patent despair of the people was underwritten by the realization that Jamaica had not served as a site for the resurgence of a mass political movement: 'Garvey had gambled on Jamaica as his strategic base from which to rebuild the movement and had lost' [Hill b p10].

Seemingly indefatigable, Garvey moved from party politics to union involvement. In 1930 he formed the Jamaican Workers and Labourers Association with himself as chairman. Garvey had been involved in the banana loaders dispute of the previous year when he acted as negotiator between the workers and the United Fruit Company management. The Workers and Labourers Association was a natural progression from informal union involvement to a programme designed to organize the workers on a mass scale; the notion of collective action was fundamental to all of Garvey's plans. But the wane of Garvey's influence brought about a reversion in his political outlook. The militant nationalism of his American years had gone. No longer did Garvey organize people in the cause of black autonomy; now he perceived his followers as a pressure group to back his representations to the colonial government for social change. Shortly after its formation, Garvey led a deputation of the Workers and Labourers Association to the Governor of Jamaica...

> ...asking him to investigate the distressing conditions of the masses of the island, and to use his influence towards remedial measures. Nonchalantly the Governor replied that in his opinion there was "no unusual suffering".
>
> [Jacques Garvey b p282]

Garvey's rediscovered reformism eventually brought him into conflict with the growing trade union movement which he had helped to launch. Several of the union leaders during Trinidad's labour crises of 1937-8 were either former Garveyites or UNIA sympathizers. Arthur Cipriani, head of the Trinidad Workingmen's Association, intervened with the colonial opposition, to permit Garvey's entry to Trinidad in 1937. Once there, however, Garvey succeeded in alienating himself from the militant wing of the workers' movement. His avowed support for Cipriani, as against the leader of the breakaway union, disappointed left-wing Trinidadians, who had expected greater radicalism of him. Although Garvey refuted allegations that he was a 'capitalist stooge', his stand on the labour issue mirrored that taken by the colonial government.

At the seventh UNIA convention, held in Kingston in 1934, the decision was taken to move headquarters to London. Accordingly, Marcus, Amy Jacques and their two sons set up home in West Kensington, London, the following year. Garvey also transferred publication of the *Black Man* to England, a monthly journal which he had begun in 1933 to replace the defunct *Negro World*. Owing to a lack of financial backing, the *Black Man's* appearances were irregular – but that Garvey managed to publish it at all was a remarkable feat.

The last years of Garvey's life were spent in London. Although he struggled valiantly to maintain his political standing, his days as a leader were over. From the soap-box on Lenox Avenue where he had inspired a millions strong movement, Garvey was reduced to a soap-box in Hyde Park where he attracted little curiosity and much animosity from a new generation of black radicals. "Today" wrote C.L.R. James in 1938, "he is a staunch supporter of the British Government and makes Tory speeches in Hyde Park about Africa, to the great annoyance of revolutionary British workers" [James b p70], Having had the misfortune to become a legend in his own lifetime, Garvey lived long enough to become a disappointment to his political successors. Just how far he had outlived his glory days was brought home to Garvey in the last, perhaps most tragic incident of his life. At the end of May, 1940, as Garvey lay ill after suffering a stroke, the world's press was wrongly notified of his death. Over the next few days Garvey endured the unenviable experience of reading his own obituaries:

> when he saw the colored American press clippings...in which the editors, in vicious glee had drawn on their own evil imaginations, he uttered a loud groan, held his head, and slumped in his chair.
>
> When he was revived and attended to by the doctor, he made signs that he wanted to dictate a message to the Press, but his speech was almost gone, and he shook with anguish at his inability to answer back his gloating enemies.
>
> (Jacques Garvey a p288]

Marcus Garvey died days later at the age of 53.

Garvey died in disappointment. He lived to see black men forget the lesson of history and once again enlist to fight another European war for democracy. He died before the anti-colonial backlash following the Second World War came to fruition with independence, as the reaction to the first had once looked set to do. He lived to see his following decline from six million to a few thousand, but died before the resurgence of interest in his work and ideas made Marcus Garvey a household name once more. Another twenty years and he could have read his harshest critics' tributes of respect to him: C.L.R. James, George Padmore, W.E.B. Du Bois and others. But his ignominious end in a lonely West Kensington flat came too soon for Garvey to witness the re-awakening of his political dreams.

The Politics of Garveyism

I shall teach the black man to see beauty in himself.
[Marcus Garvey[8]]

The United States Bureau of Investigation thought Garvey was a communist. More than one modern historian has called him a fascist. Marxists have despaired at Garvey's nationalist fervour and right-wing leanings. Garvey himself, at different points in his career, labelled his politics radical, fascist and Zionist. Throughout his life, and long after his death, contradiction and controversy have raged over the exact meaning of Garveyism – how its political philosophy is to be defined and where its political allegiances lay. The business of politically defining Garveyism is further complicated by Garvey's own development and changes, which led him in a number of different political directions over the years. Much of what is commonly thought to be meant by Garveyism is in actuality only representative of the American years of the movement. Garvey's early years in Jamaica and England were marked by a fundamentally different political outlook from the middle period in which the UNIA took America by storm. In simple terms, Garvey's politics moved from radical reformist to revolutionary to reformist. It is this broad scope of perspectives which enables seemingly contradictory definitions of Garveyism to be simultaneously correct.

Although Garvey wavered between radicalism and reformism as he moved from Jamaica to America and back again, his ideas were always underwritten by the belief that black people's subjugation was inextricably linked with colonialism in Africa. In this, the early Pan-Africanists were clearly influential on Garvey's thinking. In Garvey's view, while Africa – the homeland of black people – remained colonized and black people around the globe had no land to call their own, the world would treat them with contempt. He therefore saw the redemption of Africa as a black people's priority. But, and this can be interpreted either as Garvey's total self-identification with Africa, or as symptomatic of his absorption of Western ideologies concerning Africa's 'backwardness', he regarded Africans as distinctly incapable of liberating themselves. Thus, his plan was to oust white colonial rule and replace it with colonization by 'civilized' Western blacks. In order to achieve this, Afro-Americans needed money and skills, and so the UNIA functioned as both a promoter of business and an educationalist organization. The Negro Factories Corporation and the Black Star Line were the beginnings of Garvey's project to develop a black economic system to produce the capital for Africa's liberation. The Black Cross Nurses, African Legion, and Universal Africa Motor Corps were established as training groups for the skilled workers needed to emancipate and then govern Africa.

The fickle allegiance of the American Communist Party and the International Workers of the World to black political groups during the 1920s, left Garvey with a faint interest in communism which turned to rabid dislike after Lenin's death in 1924. Lenin had supported independent nationalist struggles as an important step in the direction of international socialism;

> It is perfectly clear that in the impending decisive battles in the world revolution, the movement of the population of the globe, initially directed towards national liberation, will turn against capitalism and imperialism and will perhaps play a much more revolutionary part than we expect.
>
> [Lenin p481]

Garvey was a great admirer of Lenin, and sent a telegram to Moscow on hearing of his death "expressing the sorrows and condolences of the 400,000,000 Negroes of the world," [in Cronon p197]. However, a growing trend in Marxist thought was consolidated in 1928 when the Sixth Comintern redecided communist policy on the nationalist issue, and specifically attacked Garvey's approach.

> Garveyism, at one time the ideology of the American Negro petty bourgeoisie and workers, and still with a certain influence over the Negro masses today, impeded the movement of these masses towards a revolutionary position...This dangerous ideology, without a single democratic feature, which toys with the aristocratic attributes of a non-existent 'Negro Kingdom', must be vigorously resisted, for it does not promote but hampers the struggle for the Negro masses for liberation from American imperialism.
>
> [in Lewis pp130-1]

This theoretical line informed the criticisms made by Garvey's Marxist opponents in Europe and America, and ended the fragile alliance which Garvey had maintained with Leninism. That American intelligence agencies continued to regard Garvey as a communist agitator, was reflective of an inability to interpret collective action as anything other than communist in the mounting hysteria of America's 'red threat' malaise.

Whether as a reaction to the withdrawal of tacit communist endorsement for his plans, or as a natural development in his economic strategy, Garvey, by the mid 1920s, was embracing capitalism with characteristic enthusiasm;

> Capitalism is necessary to the progress of the world, and those who unreasonably and wantonly oppose or fight against it are enemies to human advancement.
>
> [Garvey b p72]

Garvey's faith in capitalism proved more long lasting than his brush with communism. He was rapidly sold on his own interpretation of the American Dream; a vision to turn Africa into a capitalist success story. Garvey envisaged the creation of black capital as a means of emulating white America's international power and world prestige. The degree to which Garvey foresaw the African future in the American model is revealed in a poetic prediction, written in Atlanta prison – "Hail United States of Africa!" was Garvey's opening line [in Jacques Garvey a p169].

Garvey's plans for African colonization earned him the misleading but enduring label of the 'Back to Africa man'. At no point in his political career, however, did he ever proscribe a wholesale return to the homeland. In Garvey's scheme of things such a move would in any case be unnecessary. For once all African countries had achieved independence, black people everywhere would have world respect as social and economic equals. "African redemption," explained Amy Jacques Garvey, "is an outlet by which the race will develop and expand to the stature of men and women with national prestige and economic security, thus enhancing the position of those who remain in America to fight for full citizenship rights," [Jacques Garvey a p267]. The philosophy behind Garvey's slogan "Africa for the Africans, those at home and those abroad", is beautifully explained in the account of a Los Angeles Garveyite;

> Mr Garvey never did advocate for all Negroes to go back to Africa. [No], he never did do that. He was teaching the people that as long as you're in somebody else's house you can't rule. And if you want to rule you must have one of your own. So he was teaching the Negroes that Africa was the only continent in which they

could have a government of their own. And he made them feel that way, you see. That's what created the misunderstanding among the people. They was afraid he wanted to send them back to Africa. He said, "No, you who are here, stay here, but help to build up Africa." Just like the Jews are Israel.

[in Tolbert p100]

The analogy of Garveyism with Zionism is a common and essentially correct one. Both movements evolved amongst displaced minority groups which perceived the creation of their own nations as a solution to the state discrimination and personal prejudice they were faced with. Garveyites noted the similarities and looked to Africa for their Palestine. Garvey himself was probably unfamiliar with the theoretical concepts of Zionism, although he occasionally used the term to describe his movement. If it were possible to envisage the successful achievement of the UNIA's aims, it might be interesting to speculate whether Garvey's Africa would have mirrored Zionist Israel and also found itself condemned by the United Nations as 'a form of racism and racial domination'[9]. As it was, Garveyism's Zionist ideals remained aspirational, with neither the funding nor the mainstream political support to make them realistically achievable.

Another widespread comparison made with Garveyism is fascism. Garvey's own assertions lend weight to the claim that his movement had fascist leanings. "We were the first Fascists," he reputedly told a friend,

We had disciplined men, woman and children in training for the liberation of Africa. The black masses saw that in this extreme nationalism lay their only hope and readily supported it. Mussolini copied Fascism from me...

[in Cronon pp198-9]

In criticism of those who draw links between Garveyism and fascism, one writer has accused them of being unable to visualize 'a black nationalism which was neither reactionary or demagogic' [Vincent p16]. However, Garvey himself appeared unable to envisage black nationalism in any other terms. Judged by the criteria commonly thought to constitute a fascist ideology, reactionism and demagogy amongst them, Garvey can clearly be seen to have come close to a fascist outlook during the American phase of his career. His beliefs in economic self-sufficiency, extreme nationalism, militarist organization, elite rule under an authoritarian leader (himself), and virulent anti-communism were all characteristic of fascism. So too was his rejection of the values and institutions of liberal democracy which placed him in opposition to black civil rights campaigners (Garvey, like Malcolm X after him, would have had little time for Martin Luther King). The relation between fascism's racism and Garvey's racial purism is less clear cut. For although Garvey's philosophy of racial purity and unity never amounted to a doctrine of racial supremacy, fascism has in any case utilized racism as an optional extra rather than a fundamental component. Garvey's leadership of the UNIA was unarguably demagogic, and in his role as the Provisional President of Africa he no doubt imagined his future rule in the same vein. "Leadership means everything," he once said, "pain, blood, death" [Garvey b p9], and although he never stated it, the notion that everything needed leadership – liberation, revolution, unionization – was implicit in his thinking.

However, the close match of some Garveyite principles with certain fascist doctrines leads to a definition of Garveyism as fascism which does not fully recognize the complexities of either. African nationalism, to generations of black activists before and after Garvey, was a reaction to colonialism. It was not the xenophobically induced striving for national pride of fascism, but an answer to the oppression endured under the colonial rule of Africa by the European powers. Garvey's anti-communism resulted from his relationship with the American Communist Party rather than any theoretical disillusionment and rejection. The UNIA's economic development programme owed more to the ideas of the great reformist Booker T Washington, than to any of the progenitors of fascism's autarkic, corporist economic policies. At times so clearly a product of his colonial childhood, Garvey's attraction to militarism was to the strength and respect symbolized by the army regalia – there were few black role models of strength and respect on the scale that Garvey wanted, and even fewer symbols that would have so recognizably demonstrated the UNIA's determination to mean business. Garvey's vision of African redemption was of an economic rather than military take over. And if its subsequent government was to be under the leadership of suitably educated black people, then this was in the tradition of the colonial ideology of European democracy, and not especially an aspect of fascism. Ultimately, it must be remembered that Garvey's self-proclaimed fascism came at a time before the word had acquired its connotations of brutality, violence, and racist genocide. Like any other historic figure, Garvey cannot be judged by terms outside of his era.

If the UNIA's connections with Zionism were close and its link with fascism ambiguous, then its relation to other black movements of the 1920s and 30s can only be described as disastrous. From reports that the UNIA enjoyed a close working relationship with groups outside of New York City, it appears that the existing animosity was a result of Garvey rather than Garveyism. The NAACP in general, and W.E.B. Du Bois in particular, became Garvey's biggest enemies. At the 1920 UNIA convention, Garveyites waved banners bearing the slogans;

N – Nothing	U – United
A – Accomplished	N – Nothing can
A – After	I – Impede your
C – Considerable	A – Aspirations
P – Pretence	

[Hill d p647]

Garvey's hostility towards Du Bois stemmed in part from his feelings of educational inadequacy in the face of the NAACP's intellectualism, but primarily from his projection of the Caribbean's colour-stratification onto the American scene. Theoretical differences were only a runner-up in Garvey's attacks on the NAACP (although primary in Du Bois' rejection of the UNIA). Garvey denounced the light-skinned Du Bois as "a hater of dark people" and the NAACP as a white-aspirationist organization – "one could hardly tell whether it was a white show or a coloured vaudeville" he said of them [Garvey b p311]. He accused Du Bois – the "unfortunate mulatto" – of valuing only his white ancestry and of considering blackness to be "hideous and monstrous". Garvey made similar claims in his retaliation against the "Committee of Eight" (two of whom were prominent NAACP members). To Garvey's mind the links between near whiteness and anti-blackness were patent, and he judged the following postscript to be self-explanatory in his bid to uncover the eight's hatred of him;

> The signers of the letter to the Attorney-General are nearly all Octoroons and Quadroons. Two are black Negroes, who have married Octoroons.One is a Mulatto and Socialist, a self-styled Negro leader, who had expressed his intention of marrying a white woman but was subsequently prevented from doing so by the criticisms of the UNIA. With this lone exception all of the others are married to Octoroons.
>
> [Garvey b p308]

But this should not be interpreted as a hatred of light-skinned blacks in themselves; after all, Garvey's second marriage was to a woman of mixed, black and white parentage. What Garvey despised was the rejection of blackness which his experiences in Jamaica had taught him to associate with so-called quadroons, mulattoes and so on. Similarly, he could not see the National Association for the Advancement of *Colored* People as an organization working for black interests, when the very term 'coloured', for him, had anti-black connotations.

In his emphasis on black pride, and fuelled by his conception of 'mixed race' people as lacking in it, Garvey took a stand for racial purity and against miscegenation which came perilously close to white supremacist ideology. A controversy over whether or not Garvey supported the Ku Klux Klan was sparked off by Garvey's own statements such as this;

> Between the Ku Klux Klan and the ... National Association for the Advancement of 'Coloured' People group, give me the Klan for their honesty of purpose towards the Negro.
>
> [Garvey b p71]

The debate came to a head at the 1924 convention, when Garvey was called upon to publicly refute any allegiance to the Klan, and announce himself opposed to their principles and practices. This placed Garveyites in a difficult position, since clearly a Ku Klux Klan reaction against Garveyites in the South would be inevitable, and 'Garvey and his followers would be committing suicide to declare war on them' [Jacques Garvey a p145]. His consequent compromise – a condemnation of Ku Klux Klan 'alleged' atrocities – failed to end the controversy.

Garvey found the allegation that he was a Klan supporter incomprehensible, but it is unsurprising that few could follow the logic of his thinking which held a white supremacist organization of more value to his cause than other black organizations. That logic lay in the common theoretical ground between Garveyism and the white supremacists; the two movements overlapped in their opposition to racial amalgamation. To Garvey and the Ku Klux Klan, the NAACP's civil rights campaigns wants us all to become white by amalgamation," Garvey insisted [Garvey b p323]. And where the Klan envisaged a 'mongrelized' white race, Garvey saw a rejection of black pride and a crawling towards nearer whiteness. For Garvey it was an issue which came down to white honesty against black hypocrisy. To his critics, it was more like a psychological derange-ment and, whatever its causes, a massive political error. Under the headline "Lunatic or Traitor?" Du Bois raged against Garvey's admiration of the Ku Klux Klan's 'honesty of purpose';

> Marcus Garvey is, without a doubt, the most dangerous enemy of the Negro race in America and the world.
>
> [in Cronon p190]

Public condemnation of Garvey by other black Americans had become important during the decline and fall of the Black Star Line. The NAACP was anxious to deflect any criticism of Garvey as a black man from seeping their way. They feared a backlash against all black activists when, as they rightly foresaw, Garvey's bubble burst and the authorities moved into stamp out his Association.

> It is within this context that the Harlem leadership's hysterical reaction to Marcus Garvey must be understood. he appeared a fool, impractical, a charlatan, and as his movement foundered in financial and legal straits, it became essential to black intellectuals that the public know the difference between a showman and the real thing.
>
> [Huggins P141]

But to those whom Garveyism appealed were those without political reputations to lose – millions of ordinary black people across America. The Harlem intellectuals had as much, maybe more to say than Garvey; what they lacked were Garvey's audiences, Garvey's following, and the UNIA's membership.

But those to whom Garveyism appealed were those without political reputations to lose – millions of ordinary black people across America. The Harlem intellectuals had as much, maybe more to say than Garvey; what they lacked were Garvey's audiences, Garvey's following, and the UNIA's membership.

How Garvey attracted such enormous support was due both to what he said and the way he said it. His vision of African redemption had a duality which satisfied everybody; when Africa is ours, he preached, those who want to go can go, those who want to stay will have a better life in America. Some responded to the idea of returning to the homeland – "a place in the sun" [Garvey b p68]. Others, like Malcolm X's father, embraced the notion of economic independence for black people. Still more were inspired by Garvey's 'go it alone' approach; not pleading for change, not asking for help, but waging an autonomous fight for freedom and equality in a hostile world. The way Garvey delivered his dreams and promises was as influential as the ideas themselves. No one could match Garvey's oratorical style; his speeches were masterpieces of political rhetoric. Nor did anyone else use newspapers and journals so effectively. "Always remember that the press is a mighty power" said Garvey [*Black Man* July 1935]. Hundreds of thousands of people learned about Garveyism through the *Negro World,* and all the paper's profits were channelled into distributing it around the world. Copies left the press in New York City to take Garvey's messages to African towns and villages..C.L.R. James recorded Jomo Kenyatta's recollection of the impact the *Negro World* made;

> In 1921, Kenya nationalists unable to read would gather round a reader of Garvey's newspaper, the *Negro World,* and listen to an article two or three times. Then they would run various ways through the forest carefully to repeat the whole, which they had memorized, to Africans hungry for some doctrine which lifted them from the servile consciousness in which Africans lived.
>
> [James a p397]

However much in disagreement with his views, no one can deny that Garvey's means of putting them across were magnificently effective. To quote C.L.R. James again, who was largely unimpressed by either Garveyism or Garvey;

> When you bear in mind the slenderness of his resources, the vast material forces and the pervading social conceptions which automatically sought to destroy him, his achievement remains one of the propagandistic miracles of this century.
>
> [James c p396]

No analysis of Garvey's political philosophy could ever be simple. In his lifetime, political issues became confused with personality clashes and power struggles. Since his death, the complexities have continued as a range of historians have brought their own political persuasions to bear on their definitions of Garveyism, resulting in a myriad of interpretations from an 'egomaniac' with 'fascist leanings' to 'anti-colonial champion'. Garvey himself, with his wide range of interests and equally broad espousal of differing political approaches, bears out almost any political label attached to him. Ultimately, he represents a nightmare to political science theoreticians, who have tried to squeeze him into the boundaries of existing dogmas and found nowhere in which he exactly fits.

The Legacy of Garveyism

'No one knows when the hour of Africa's redemption cometh. It is in the wind. It is coming. One day, like a storm, it will be here.'
(Marcus Garvey[10])

It has been commonly thought of Marcus Garvey that he said a great deal but 'achieved little in the way of permanent improvement for his people' [Cronon p4]. In terms of Garvey's own goals, he certainly failed; Africa still belonged to the Europeans at the time of his death, and black people in the United States continued to live as second class citizens. But Garvey set in motion something far more enduring than his African colonization project, something which has achieved more in the way of permanent improvement for black people than the ideas of any other man or woman. The formation of the political consciousness which has given black people a new base from which to fight against their racist oppression, owes much to Garvey. Although Garvey did not create them, and did little to develop them, he took the emergent theories of black consciousness out of the hands of the closeted intellectuals and delivered them to the people. Without Garvey's popularization, the concepts of black pride, black solidarity, and blackness as an organizing principle in the collectivization of resistance to racism, would have remained no more than abstract notions. Garvey gave millions of black people an awareness of their shared history and common interests. The improvements which black people have made for themselves in the decades since his death are all a part of Garvey's legacy to the world.

"Every time you see another nation on the African continent become independent," Malcolm X is reported to have said, "you know that Marcus Garvey is alive." [in Jacques Garvey a p307] Many of those involved in the African nationalist struggles for independence, acknowledged their debt to Garvey for the inspiration he gave to

their fight. "Is Mau Mau the hand of Marcus Garvey?" asked the
Chicago *Defender* in 1953, and in spirit at least, to Jomo Kenyatta's
compatriots who had avidly read the *Negro World* during the 1920s,
it probably was. Kenyatta, who became the first Prime Minister of
self-governing Kenya in August, 1963, considered himself a member
of the UNIA and claimed to have been converted to the philosophy
"Africa for the Africans" after meeting Garvey. Kwame Nkrumah,
the man who oversaw Ghana's transition to independence, honoured the 'sons and daughters' of the African diaspora:

> Many of them made no small contribution to the cause of African freedom. A
> name that springs immediately to mind in this connection is Marcus Garvey.
> Long before many of us were even conscious of our own degradation, Marcus
> Garvey fought for African national and racial equality.
>
> [in Jacques Garvey a p319]

The first Presidents of independent Zambia and Zaire, Dr Kuanda
and Colonel Mobutu, both made public their admiration for Garvey
and gratitude to his teachings. In a legendary story of Garvey's
renown throughout Africa, it was said that...

> The King of Swaziland told a friend some years after that he knew the names of
> only two black men in the Western world, Jack Johnson and Marcus Garvey.
>
> [James b p68]

Garvey was both right and wrong in his view that African liberation
was only achievable with the aid of black economic support. The
African battles for independence were fought and won without it.
But the freedom they have gained from colonial rule has done little
to end their subjugation under the yoke of imperialist exploitation.
The greater number of the African countries now play underdog in a
world economic system which, in the fulfilment of its historical
evolution, benefits the Western nations at their expense. Garvey's
dream of Africa's redemption to interntional equality looks further
away than ever, as its status has dropped from second class society
to Third World continent. Garvey's generation located black people's
oppression in the continuation of colonialism. With the benefit of
hindsight, black radicals of the post-colonial era have seen that
colonialism merely consolidated the racist trend in Europe's treatment of blacks and its removal has changed nothing in that
conception. Most of Africa is free, the struggle in Azania continues;
but freedom from the political rule of settler-colonialism has not
amounted to liberation from the on-going economic involvement of
the erstwhile colonizers. Africa still does not truly belong to the
Africans.

A new generation of black militants were born into Garveyite households in the 1920s and 30s, to take the renascent black struggle to its American peak in the 1950s and 1960s. The achievements of those decades were more tangible than any of Garvey's era, but the new movements were built on the foundations of political activism which Garvey had laid. Even the ideological rifts between the 1960s campaigners had their roots in earlier disagreements. The schism between Garvey's militant nationalism and Du Bois' equally fierce lobby for change, was later parallelled by Malcolm X's Islamic nationalism and Martin Luther King's Civil Rights movement; two on-going solutions to the continuing problem of racism. Where Martin Luther King was the spiritual descendant of Garvey rather than Du Bois, was in the strategy of mass action; whereby the optimism of the decade motivated marches above and beyond the scale of the UNIA, but firmly in its tradition.

The Black Muslims were born directly of the UNIA. Their founder, Elijah Mohammed, had been a member in the Chicago division, and their greatest spokesman, Malcolm X, grew up in a Garveyite family. Malcolm X took care to acknowledge the influence of Garveyism upon the movement:

> All the freedom movements that are taking place right here in America today were initiated by the work and teachings of Marcus Garvey. The entire Black Muslim philosophy here in America is feeding upon the seeds that were planted by Marcus Garvey.
>
> [in Jacques Garvey a p308]

And although Martin Luther King's Civil Rights movement was more the successor of the NAACP, King recognized that the popularization of black action owed its greatest debt to Garvey. Speaking to a crowd at the Jamaican National Stadium in 1965, he stated:

> You gave Marcus Garvey to the United States of America, and he gave to the millions of Negroes in the United States a sense of personhood, a sense of manhood and a sense of somebodiness.
>
> [ibid]

Whether black Americans marched on Washington with King, or prayed to Allah with Malcolm X, or armed themselves with the Black Panthers, or simply came to see that 'black is beautiful', they all embodied the legacy of Garveyism. Garvey's messages were re-expressed to become the demands of Black Power, and the Garvey instilled 'sense of somebodiness' carried them through.

As the African liberation struggles and black American militancy of the 1960s were reminding the world about Marcus Garvey, the people of Jamaica were reclaiming him as their hero. There is a certain ambiguity in Jamaica's official adulation of Garvey who, after all, had felt bitterly let down by the Jamaican people. With a degree of cynicism, a Jamaican biographer of Garvey writes of the island's reaction to the decision that his body would be removed from London and reinterred in Jamaica:

> At the time of the announcement Garvey was the 'Negro leader', then he was gradually transformed into the 'Jamaican patriot' and by the time his body arrived in Jamaica he had become the 'Jamaica hero.'
>
> [Edwards p37]

However, there were thousands of loyal Garvey supporters who had never forgotten their leader, and considered him their National Hero long before the government officially made him one. Garvey's statue in Kingston's main park, unveiled in 1956, and Garvey's reinterrment in Jamaican soil, in 1964, made no difference to his standing in their eyes. Garveyites had continued the tradition of grassroots activism which Garvey had established in Jamaica. Both of his former wives – Amy Ashwood and Amy Jacques Garvey – were involved in the People's National Party, founded by Norman Manley (who, incidentally, had been the lawyer advising the municipal council's decision to remove Garvey from office in 1930), and which took government in 1953. The People's National Party's political programme was not dissimilar to that which the People's Political Party had launched decades earlier.

Amongst the figures of Jamaica's officialdom, there are few whose veneration of Garvey was ever matched by interest in his political views. A notable exception is Alexander Bustamente, the trade union leader who became the first Prime Minister of post-colonial Jamaica. Bustamente lectured on Garvey's work to union members, stressing his pioneering efforts in labour unionization. In the main though, there is an irony in the canonization of Garvey – a very black, black man – by a leadership which continues to this day to be dominated by the light skinned black people Garvey was so politically hostile to. There is a sense of the politics of Garveyism somehow being mislaid in the official recognition of Garvey. For a historian writing in the early 1970s, this feeling is strengthened by the fact that 'Jamaica reveres the memory of Marcus Garvey, who is safely dead, but bans the writings of Malcolm X, Stokely Carmichael and Frantz Fanon' [Lowenthal p313]. But if Garveyism has been virtually depoliticized in Jamaica's tributes to Garvey then this represents one stand in the duality of Garvey's contribution to the modern black world. He gave his politics – to be taken or left – and he gave himself – another impressive figure to the list of black achievers. Successive generations of Jamaican officials have admired the latter and rejected the former; many of today's foremost black thinkers have done the same.

Simultaneous to the Jamaican government's commemoration of the memory of Garvey there has occurred, also in Jamaica, the most literal development of Garveyism into the present time. The originators of the Rastafari movement were from the rank and file of Kingston's UNIA division. The spiritual foundations of Rastafarianism lie in Garvey's 'Back to Africa' philosophy, and Garvey is regarded as the greatest modern prophet of the movement. Rastafarianism, however, has involved only the appropriation of certain aspects of Garveyism; primarily, the notion of return for the peoples of the African exodus. Garvey himself had a somewhat ambivalent attitude towards Haile Selassie – the Rastafarian messiah – who he supported as the leader of Africa's only uncolonized nation, but refused to accept as the messianic leader of black people. When Mussolini's Italian army invaded Ethiopia in 1935, and Haile Selassie fled to the safety of London, Garvey attacked the Emperor's actions in *Black Man* editorials. Whilst condemning the Italian action, he considered Selassie to have contributed to Ethiopia's downfall by a lack of proper defence and a failure to seek international black support.

> If Haile Selassie had negotiated the proper relationship with the hundreds of millions of Negroes outside of Abyssinia in Africa, in South and Central America, in the United States of America, in Canada, the Westindies and Australia, he could have had an organization of men and women ready to do service, not only in the development of Abyssinia as a great Negro nation, but on the spur of the moment to protect it from any foe.
>
> [Black Man, July-August 1936]

This was the exact role which Garvey had envisaged for the UNIA (a much depleted organization by this time), as he clearly believed in pragmatic manouevres rather than implicit faith in the guidance of God – "He resorted sentimentally to prayer," he said of Selassie [Black Man, January 1937]. However, it was a message, undocumented but attributed to Garvey, which led to the Rastafarians' choice of Selassie as the God of Ethiopia; 'Look to Africa when a black king shall be crowned for the day of deliverance is near' [in Cashmore p5]

Since the 1970s, the Rastafarian movement has grown in size and importance in Jamaica and, increasingly, in Britain's inner-cities amongst black people perceiving themselves to be twice displaced from their African homeland. Rastafarianism's physical return to Africa ideal is drawn from Garvey's teachings but is not strictly in accordance with his meanings. As Amy Jacques Garvey explained, 'There was no back-to-Africa movement except in a spiritual sense.' [in Essein-Udom p66]. Today, Rastas embody abstracted Garveyism in its purest form, and the continued social marginalization and fierce criticism from the Jamaican authorities which they experience, further testify to the absence of Garvey's politics in his official veneration.

The forms in which Garveyism has lived on have been diverse; from nationalist fighters in Kenya, to bronze statues in Kingston, or from Black Power militants in Birmingham, Alabama to Rastfarians living in Birmingham, England. All of these are attributable in no small way to the work of Marcus Garvey. More than this, though, in the struggle up from degradation and subjugation, Garvey contributed to the popularization of black consciousness, and his greatest living tribute are the millions of black people around the world who might never have said "I'm black and proud" without him. In the unfinished history of black people's fight against the oppression of racism, Marcus Garvey's contribution towards the inevitable victory is immeasurable.

NOTES

1. Garvey b p1

2. cited by Garvey in a public speech, Garvey a

3. Garvey b p11

4. Garvey was probably unaware of the meaning of 'Imperialism' when he included this in the UNIA's original programme; it was dropped in the UNIA's revision of its aims and principles in 1920.

5. Garvey b p14

6. Garvey b p9

7. Garvey b p101

8. cited in Edwards p27

9. A resolution condemning Zionism as 'a form of racism and racial domination' was carried at the U.N. General Assembly by 72 votes to 35 (with 32 abstentions), on November 10, 1975.

10. Garvey b p10

BIBLIOGRAPHY

CASHMORE, E.E. *The Rastafarians,* Minority Rights Group, Report no. 64, 1984.

CLARKE, J.H. ed., *Marcus Garvey and the Vision of Africa,* Vintage Books, New York, 1974.

CRONON, E.D., *Black Moses: The story of Marcus Garvey and the Universal Negro Improvement Association,* University of Wisconsin Press, Wisconsin, 2nd edn., 1969.

DENNIS, D., and WILLMARTH, S., *Black History for Beginners,* Writers and Readers, London, 1984.

EDWARDS, A., *Marcus Garvey: 1887-1940,* New Beacon Books, London, 1967.

ESSEIN-UDOM, E.U., *Black Nationalism: The Rise of the Black Muslims in the U.S.A.,* Penguin, Harmondsworth, 1962.

FRYER, P., *Staying Power,* Pluto Press, London, 1984.

GARVEY, M., (a) *Minutes of Proceedings of the Speech by The Hon. Marcus Garvey, at the Century Theatre, Archer Street, Westbourne Grove, London, September, 1928,* UNIA, London.
(b) *Philosophy and Opinions of Marcus Garvey, vols. I & II,* A. Jacques Garvey ed., Antheneum, New York, 1974.

GUY, R., *A Measure of Time,* Virago, London, 1984.

HILL, R., (a) 'The first English years and after, 1912-16', in Clarke, pp38-70.
(b) ed., and introduction to *The Black Man, 1933-39,* Kraus-Thompson, New York, 1975.
(c) ed. *The Marcus Garvey and Universal Negro Improvement Association Papers, Volume I, 1826-August 1919,* University of California Press, California, 1983.
(d) ed. *The Marcus Garvey and Universal Negro Improvement Association Papers, Volume II, 27 August 1919-31 August 1920,* University of California Press, California, 1983.

HUGGINS, N.I., *Harlem Rennaissance,* Oxford University Press, London, 1971.

JACQUES GARVEY, A., (a) *Garvey and Garveyism,* Macmillan, New York, 1970.
(b) 'The Political Activities of Marcus Garvey in Jamaica' in Clarke, pp276-283.

JAMES, C.L.R., (a) *The Life of Captain Cipriani,* Lancashire, 1932.
(b) *A History of Negro Revolt,* Haskell House, 1938.
(c) *The Black Jacobins,* Vintage Books, New York, 1965.

LENIN, V.I. *Collected Works,* Volume 32, Progress Publishers, Moscow, 1973.

LEWIS, R. and WARNER-LEWIS, M., eds. *Garvey: Africa, Europe, the Americas,* University of the Westindies, Jamaica, 1986.

LEWIS, R., *Marcus Garvey: Anti-Colonial Champion,* Karia Press, London, 1987.

LOWENTHAL, D., *West Indian Societies,* Oxford University Press, London, 1972.

LYNCH, H.R., *Edward Wilmot Blyden: Pan Negro Patriot,* Oxford University Press, New York, 1967.

MAY, R., and COHEN, R., 'The Interaction between Race and Colonialism: A Case Study of the Liverpool Race Riots of 1919', *Race and Class,* XVI, 1974-5.

TOLBERT, E.J., *The UNIA and Black Los Angeles,* Centre for Afro-American Studies, University of California, 1980.

VINCENT, T.G., *Black Power and the Garvey Movement,* Ramparts Press, California, 5th edn., 1976.

WILLIAMS, K.M., *The Rastafarians,* Ward Lock Educational, London, 1981.

PART II

Articles and Speeches by Marcus Garvey

1. The Negro's Greatest Enemy

I was born in the Island of Jamaica, British Westindies, on Aug. 17, 1887.My parents were black negroes. My father was a man of brilliant intellect and dashing courage. He was unafraid of consequences. He took human chances in the course of life, as most bold men do, and he failed at the close of his career. He once had a fortune; he died poor. My mother was a sober and conscientious Christian, too soft and good for the time in which she lived. She was the direct opposite of my father. He was severe, firm, determined, bold and strong, refusing to yield even to superior forces if he believed he was right. My mother, on the other hand, was always willing to return a smile for a blow, and ever ready to bestow charity upon her enemy. Of this strange combination I was born thirty-six years ago, and ushered into a world of sin, the flesh and [d] the devil.

I grew up with other black and white boys. I was never whipped by any, but made them all respect the strength of my arms. I got my education from many sources – through private tutors, two public schools, two grammar or high schools and two colleges. My teachers were men and women of varied experiences and abilities; four of them were eminent preachers. They studied me and I studied them. With some I became friendly in after years, others and I drifted apart, because as a boy they wanted to whip me, and I simply refused to be whipped. I was not made to be whipped. It annoys me to be defeated; hence to me, to be once defeated is to find cause for an everlasting struggle to reach the top.

I became a printer's apprentice at an early age, while still attending school. My apprentice master was a highly educated and alert man. In the affairs of business and the world he had no peer. He taught me many things before I reached twelve, and at fourteen I had enough intelligence and experience to manage men. I was strong and manly, and I made them respect me. I developed a strong and forceful character, and have maintained it still.

To me, at home in my early days, there was no difference between white and black. One of my father's properties, the place where I lived most of the time, was adjoining that of a white man. He had three girls and two boys; the Wesleyan minister, another white man whose church my parents attended, also had property adjoining ours. He had three girls and one boy. All of us were playmates. We romped and were happy children playmates together. The little girl whom I liked most knew no better than I did myself. We were two innocent fools who never dreamed of a race feeling and problem. As a child, I went to school with white boys and girls, like all other negroes. We were not called negroes then. I never hea[r]d the term negro used once until I was about fourteen.

At fourteen my little white playmate and I parted. Her parents thought the time had come to separate us and draw the colour line. They sent her and another sister to Edinburgh, Scotland, and told her that she was never to write or try to get in touch with me, for I was a "nigger". It was then that I found for the first time that there was some difference in humanity, and that there were different races, each having its own separate and distinct social life. I did not care about the separation after I was told about it, because I never thought all during our childhood association that the girl and the rest of the children of her race were better than I was; in fact, they used to look up to me. So I simply had no regrets. I only thought them "fresh"

After my first lesson in race distinction, I never thought of playing with white girls any more, even if they might be next door neighbours. At home my sister's company was good enough for me,and at school I made friends with the coloured girls next to me. White boys and I used to frolic together. We played cricket and baseball, ran races and rode bicycles together, took each other to the river and to the sea beach to learn to swim, and made boyish efforts while out in the deep water to drown each other, making a sprint for shore crying out "shark, shark, shark." In all our experiences, however, only one black boy was drowned. He went under on a Friday afternoon after school hours, and his parents found him afloat half eaten by sharks on the following Sunday afternoon. Since then we boys never went back to sea.

"YOU ARE BLACK"

At maturity the black and white boys separated, and took different courses in life. I grew up to then see the difference between the races more and more. My schoolmates as young men did not know or remember me any more. Then I realized that I had to make a fight for a place in the world, that it was not so easy to pass on to office and position. Personally, however, I had not much difficulty in finding and holding a place for myself, for I was aggressive. At eighteen I had an excellent position as manager of a large printing establishment having under my control several men old enough to be my grandfathers. But I got mixed up with public life. I started to take an interest in the politics of my country, and then I saw the injustice done to my race because it was black, and I became dissatisfied on that account. I went travelling to South and Central America and parts of the Westindies to find out if it was so elsewhere, and I found the same situation. I set sail for Europe to find out if it was different there, and again I found the same stumbling-block – "You are black." I read of the conditions in America. I read "Up From Slavery," by Booker T. Washington, and then my doom – if I may so call it – of being a race leader dawned upon me in London after I had traveled through almost half of Europe.

I asked, "Where is the black man's Government?" "Where is his King and his kingdom?" "Where is his President, his country, and his ambassador, his army, his navy, his men of big affairs?" I could not find them, and then I declared, "I will help to make them."

Becoming naturally restless for the opportunity of doing something [for] the advancement of my race, I was determind that the black man would not continue to be kicked about by all the other races and nations of the world, as I saw it in the Westindies, South and Central America and Europe, and as I read of it in America. My young and ambitious mind led me into flights of great imagination. I saw before me then, even as I do now, a new world of black men, not peons, serfs, dogs and slaves, but a nation of sturdy men making their impress upon civilization and causing a new light to dawn upon the human race. I could not remain in London any more. My brain was afire. There was a world of thought to conquer. I had to start ere it became too late and the work be not done. Immediately I boarded a ship at Southampton for Jamaica, where I arrived on July 15, 1914. The Universal Negro Improvement Association and African Communities (Imperial) League was founded and organized five days after my arrival, with the program of uniting all the negro peoples of the world into one great body to establish a country and Government absolutely their own.

Where did the name of the organization come from? It was while speaking to a Westindian negro who was a passenger with me from Southampton, who was returning home to the Westindies from Basutoland with his Basuto wife, that I further learned of the horrors of native life in Africa. He related to me in conversation such horrible and pitiable tales that my heart bled within me. Retiring from the conversation to my cabin, all day and the following night I pondered over the subject matter of that conversation, and at midnight, lying flat on my back, the vision and thought came to me

that I should name the organization the Universal Negro Improvement Association and African Communities (Imperial) League.
Such a name I thought would embrace the purpose of all black
humanity.Thus to the world a name was born, a movement created
and a man became known.

I really never knew there was so much colour prejudice in
Jamaica, my own native home, until I started the work of the
Universal Negro Improvement Association. We started immediately
before the war. I had just returned from a successful trip to Europe,
which was an exceptional achievement for a black man. The daily
papers wrote me up with big headlines and told of my movement.
But nobody wanted to be a negro. "Garvey is crazy; he has lost his
head," "Is that the use he is going to make of his experience and
intelligence?" – such were the criticisms passed upon me. Men and
women as black as I, and even more so, had believed themselves
white under the Westindian order of society. I was simply an
impossible man to use openly the term "negro;" yet everyone
beneath his breath was calling the black man a negro.

I had to decide whether to please my friends and be one of the
"black-whites" of Jamaica, and be reasonably prosperous, or come
out openly and defend and help improve and protect the integrity of
the black millions and suffer. I decided to do the latter, hence my
offence against "coloured-black-white" society in the colonies and
America. I was openly hated and persecuted by some of these
coloured men of the island who did not want to be classified as
negroes, but as white. They hated me worse than poison. They
opposed me at every step, but I had a large number of white friends,
who encouraged and helped me. Notable among them were the then
Governor of the Colony, the Colonial Secretary and several other
prominent men. But they were afraid of offending the "coloured
gentry" that were passing for white. Hence my fight had to be made
alone. I spent hundred of pounds (sterling) helping the organization
to gain a footing. I also gave up all my time to the promulagation of
its ideals. I became a marked man, but I was determined that the
work should be done.

The war helped a great deal in arousing the consciousness of the
coloured people to the reasonableness of our program, especially
after the British at home had rejected a large number of Westindian
coloured men who wanted to be officers in the British army. When
they were told that negroes could not be officers in the British army
they started their own propoganda, which supplemented the
program of the Universal Negro Improvement Association. With
this and other contributing agencies, a few of the stiff-necked

coloured people began to see the reasonableness of my program, but they were firm in refusing to be known as negroes. Furthermore, I was a black man and therefore had absolutely no right to lead; in the opinion of the "coloured" element, leadership should have been made in the hands of a yellow or a very light man. On such flimsy prejudices our race has been retarded. There is more bitterness among us negroes because of the caste of colour than there is between any other peoples, not excluding the people of India.

I succeeded to a great extent in establishing the association in Jamaica with the assistance of a Catholic Bishop, the Governor, Sir John Pringle, the Rev. William Graham, a Scottish clergyman and several other white friends. I got in touch with Booker Washington and told him what I wanted to do. He invited me to America and promised to speak with me in the Southern and other States to help my work. Although he died in the Fall of 1915, I made my arrangements and arrived in the United States on March 23, 1916.

Here I found a new and different problem. I immediately visited some of the then so-called negro leaders, only to discover, after a close study of them, that they had no program, but were mere opportunists who were living off their so-called leadership while the poor people were groping in the dark. I travelled through thirty-eight States and everywhere found the same condition. I visited Tuskegee and paid my respects to the dead hero, Booker Washington, and then returned to New York, where I organized the New York Division of the Universal Negro Improvement Associaton. After instructing the people in the aims and objects of the association, I intended returning to Jamaica to perfect the Jamaica organization, but when we had enrolled about 800 or 1,000 members in the Harlem district and had elected the officers, a few negro politicians began trying to turn the movement into a political club.

POLITICAL FACTION FIGHT

Seeing that these politicians were about to destroy my ideals, I had to fight to get them out of the organization. There it was that I made my first political enemies in Harlem. They fought me until they smashed the first organization and reduced its membership to about fifty. I started again and in two months built up a new organization of about 1,500 members. Again the politicians came and divided us into factions. They took away all the books of the organization, its treasury and all its belongings. At that time I was only an organizer, for it was not then my intention to remain in America, but to return to Jamaica. The organization had its proper officers elected, and I was not an officer of the New York division, but President of the Jamaica branch.

On the second split in Harlem thirteen of the members conferred with me and requested me to become President for a time of the New York organization so as to save them from the politicians. I consented and was elected president. There then sprung up two factions, one led by the politicians with the books and the money, and the other led by me. My faction had no money. I placed at their disposal what money I had, opened an office for them, employed two women secretaries, went on the streets of Harlem at night to speak for the movement. In three weeks more than 2,000 new members joined. By this time I had the association incorporated so as to prevent the other faction using the name, but in two weeks the politicians had stolen all the people's money and had smashed up their faction.

The organization under my Presidency grew by leaps and bounds. I started *The Negro World*. Being a journalist, I edited this paper free of cost for the association, and worked for them without pay until November, 1920. I travelled all over the country for the association at my own expense, and established branches until 1919 we had about thirty branches in different cities. By my writings and speeches we were able to build up a large organization of over 2,000,000 by June 1919, at which time we launched the program of the Black Star Line.

To have built up a new organization, which was not purely political, among negroes in America is a wonderful feat, for the negro politician does not allow any other kind of organization within his race to thrive. We succeeded, however, in making the Universal Negro Improvement Association so formidable in 1919 that we encountered more trouble from our political bretheren. They sought the influence of the District Attorney's office of the County of New York to put us out of business. Edwin P. Kilroe, at that time an Assistant District Attorney, on the complaint of the negro politicians, started to investigate us and the association. Mr Kilroe would constantly and continuously call me to his office for investigation on extraneous matters without coming to the point. The result was that after the eight or ninth time I wrote an article in our newspaper, *The Negro World,* against him. This was interpreted as criminal libel, for which I was indicted and arrested, but subsequently dismissed on retracting what I had written.

During my many tilts with Mr Kilroe, the question of the Black Star Line was discussed. He did not want us to have a line of ships. I told him that even as there was a White Star Line, we would have, irrespective of his wishes, a Black Star Line. On June 27, 1919, we incorporated the Black Star Line of Delaware, and in September we obtained a ship.

The following month (October) a man by the name of Tyler came to my office at 56 West 135th Street, New York City, and told me that Mr Kilroe had sent him to "get me," and at once fired four shots at me from a .38-calibre revolver. He wounded me in the right leg and the right side of my scalp. I was taken to the Harlem Hospital and he was arrested. The next day it was reported that he committed suicide in jail just before he was taken before a City Magistrate.

RECORD-BREAKING CONVENTION

The first year of our activities for the Black Star Line added prestige to the Universal Negro Improvement Association. Several hundred thousand dollars worth of shares were sold. Our first ship, the steamship Yarmouth, had made two voyages to the Westindies and Central America. The white press had flashed the news all over the world. I, a young negro, as President of the corporation, had become famous. My name was discussed on five continents. The Universal Negro Improvement Association gained millions of followers all over the world. By August, 1920, over 4,000,000 persons had joined the movement. A convention of all the negro peoples of the world was called to meet in New York that month. Delegates came from all parts of the known world. Over 25,000 persons packed the Madison Square Garden on Aug. 1 to hear me speak to the first International Convention of Negroes. It was a record-breaking meeting, the first and the biggest of its kind. The name of Garvey had become known as a leader of his race.

Such fame among negroes was too much for other race leaders and politicians to tolerate. My downfall was planned by my enemies. They laid all kinds of traps for me. They scattered their spies among the employes [sic] of the Black Star Line and the Universal Negro Improvement Association. Our office records were stolen. Employes [sic] started to be openly dishonest; we could get no convictions against them; even if on complaint they were held by a Magistrate, they were dismissed by the Grand Jury. The ships' officers started to pile up thousands of dollars of debts against the company without the knowledge of the officers of the corporation. Our ships were damaged at sea, and there was a general riot of wreck and ruin. Officials of the Universal Negro Improvement Association also began to steal and be openly dishonest. I had to dismiss them. They joined my enemies, and thus I had an endless fight on my hands to save the ideals of the association and carry out our program for the race. My negro enemies, finding that they alone could not destroy me, resorted to misrepresenting me to the leaders of the white race, several of whom, without proper investigation, also opposed me.

With robberies from within and from without, the Black Star Line was forced to suspend active business in December, 1921. While I was on a business trip to the Westindies in the Spring of 1921, the Black Star Line received the blow from which it was unable to recover. A sum of $25,000 was paid by one of the officers of the corporation to a man to purchase a ship, but the ship was never obtained and the money was never returned. The company was defrauded of a further sum of $11,000. Through such actions on the part of dishonest men in the shipping business, the Black Star Line received its first setback. This resulted in my being indicted for using the United States mails to defraud investors in the company. I was subsequently convicted and sentenced to five years in a Federal penitentiary. My trial is a matter of history. I know I was not given a square deal, because my indictment was the result of a "frame up" among my political and business enemies. I had to conduct my own case in court because of the peculiar position in which I found myself. I had millions of friends and a large number of enemies. I wanted a coloured attorney to handle my case, but there was none I could trust. I feel that I have been denied justice because of prejudice. Yet I have an abundance of faith in the courts of America, and I hope yet to obtain justice on my appeal.

ASSOCIATION'S 6,000,000 MEMBERSHIP

The temporary ruin of the Black Star Line in no way affected the larger work of the Universal Negro Improvement Association, which now has 900 branches with an approximate membership of 6,000,000. This organization has succeeeded in organizing the negroes all over the world and we now look forward to a renaissance that will create a new people and bring about the restoration of Ethiopia's ancient glory.

Being black, I have committed an unpardonable offense against the very light coloured negroes in America and the Westindies by making myself famous as a negro leader of millions. In their view, no black man must rise above them, but I still forge ahead determined to give to the world the truth about the new negro who is determined to make and hold for himself a place in the affairs of men. The Universal Negro Improvement Association has been misrepresented by my enemies. They have tried to make it appear that we are hostile to other races. This is absolutely false. We love all humanity. We are working for the peace of the world which we believe can only come about when all races are given their due.

We feel that there is absolutely no reason why there should be any differences between the black and white races, if each stop to adjust and steady itself. We believe in the purity of both races. We do not believe the black man should be encouraged in the idea that his highest purpose in life is to marry a white woman, but we do believe that the white man should be taught to respect the black woman in the same way as he wants the black man to respect the white woman. It is a vicious and dangerous doctrine of social equality to urge, as certain coloured leaders do, that black and white should get together, for that would destroy the racial purity of both.

We believe that the black people should have a country of their own where they should be given the fullest opportunity to develop politically, socially and industrially. The black people should not be encouraged to remain in white people's countries and expect to be Presidents, Governors, Mayors, Senators, Congressmen, Judges and social and industrial leaders. We believe that with the rising ambition of the negro, if a country is not provided for him in another 50 or 100 years, there will be a terrible clash that will end disastrously to him and disgrace our civilization. We desire to prevent such a clash by pointing the negro to a home of his own. We feel that all well disposed and broad minded white men will aid in this direction. It is because of this belief no doubt that my negro enemies, so as to prejudice me further in the opinion of the public, wickedly state that I am a member of the Ku Klux Klan, even though I am a black man.

I have been deprived of the opportunity of properly explaining my work to the white people of America through the prejudice worked up against me by jealous and wicked members of my own race. My success as a[n] organizer was much more than rival negro leaders could tolerate. They, regardless of consequences, either to me or to the race, had to destroy me by fair means or foul. The thousands of anonymous and other hostile letters written to the editors and publishers of the white press by negro rivals to prejudice me in the eyes of public opinion are sufficient evidence of the wicked and vicious opposition I have had to meet from among my own people, especially among the very lightly coloured. But they went further than the press in their attempts to discredit me. They organized clubs all over the United States and the Westindies, and wrote both open and anonymous letters to city, State and Federal officials of this and other Governments to induce them to use their influence to hamper and destroy me. No wonder, therefore, that several Judges, District Attorneys and other high officials have been against me without knowing me. No wonder, therefore, that the great white population of this country and of the world has a wrong impression of the aims and objects of the Universal Negro Improvement Association and of the work of Marcus Garvey.

THE STRUGGLE OF THE FUTURE

Having had the wrong education as a start in his racial career, the negro has become his own greatest enemy. Most of the trouble I have had in advancing the cause of the race has come from negroes. Booker Washington aptly described the race in one of his lectures by stating that we were like crabs in a barrel, that none would allow the other to climb over, but on any such attempt all would continue to pull back into the barrel the one crab that would make the effort to climb out. Yet, those of us with vision cannot desert the race, leaving it to suffer and die.

Looking forward a century or two, we can see an economic and political death struggle for the survival of the different race groups. Many of our present-day national centres will have become over-crowded with vast surplus populations. The fight for bread and position will be keen and severe, the weaker and unprepared group is bound to go under. That is why, visionaries as we are in the Universal Negro Improvement Association, we are fighting for the founding of a negro nation in Africa, so that there will be no clash between black and white and that each race will have a separate existence and civilization all its own without courting suspicion and hatred or eyeing each other with jealousy and rivalry within the borders of the same country.

White men who have struggled for and built up their countries and their own civilizations are not disposed to hand them over to the negro or any other race without let or hindrance. It would be unreasonable to expect this. Hence any vain assumption on the part of the negro to imagine that he will one day become the President of the Nation, Governor of the State, or Mayor of the city in the countries of white men, is like waiting on the devil and his angels to take up their residence in the Realm on High and direct there the affairs of Paradise.

Printed in *Current History,* 18:6 (September 1923), pp 951-57

2. Address by Marcus Garvey

...Mr Chairman, ladies and gentlemen – On behalf of the Universal Negro Improvement Association I beg to lay before you the idea for establishing an Industrial Farm and Institute in the interest of our people and country and I am asking you as members, friends and sympathisers to follow me closely as I give expression to the executive feelings and desire of our society, which I feel sure will meet with your hearty approval and support. The condition of our country and people is as much known to you as it is to me, but sometimes it becomes necessary for one to draw things in picture-like illustration to remind and impress those who ought to be interested. Hence I shall take the liberty to arrest your attention for a while in pointing out, even as you do know yourselves, the existing state of affairs.

Our people have had seventy-seven years of unfettered liberty in this country – a liberty given us by the liberty-loving and Christian British people – during which period of time we have tried our best to adopt ourselves to the environments of the country and to live up to the teachings of our Christian brothers. We have nothing to regret in adopting and living up to the teachings of our more fortunate and cultured friends, for in obeying their teachings and living up to their principles we have only done the right thing to bring us on par with the civilized habits and customs of the most cultured and civilized of mankind. Thank God there is no racial friction in Jamaica and I pray that the day may never dawn to see anything of racial friction or open racial prejudice in this country. Jamaica has a lesson to teach the world, and it is that people of different races can live together within one country as brothers and friends on the best of terms without prejudice upholding one government, ready to die for one flag, enjoying the same liberty of constitution (Christian and otherwise) and looking to the common destiny.

I say thank God for this state of affairs, and it shall be the principle of the Universal Negro Improvement Association to live up to and spread the

DOCTRINE OF BROTHERHOOD AND LOVE

among all mankind all over the world. We stand on the platform of humanity, and whether the man be black, white of blue, it shall be our mission to clasp his hand in fellowship. Any man who despises another because of his race only, is mean and in everyway a coward. God made us all to dwell on the face of the earth, so whether we are this, that or the other, we are all children of one common father. With Booker T. Washington, I repeat these words of wisdom, not for the people of America, but for the people of Jamaica:

> "Different in race, in colour, in history, we can teach the world that, although thus differing, it is possible for us to dwell side by side in love, in peace, and in material prosperity. We can be one in sympathy, purpose, forbearance, and mutual happiness. Let him who would embitter, would bring strife, between your race and mine be accursed in his basket and in his store, accursed in the fruit of his body and the fruit of his land. No man can plan the degradation of another race without being himself degraded. The highest test of the civilisation of any race is its willingness to extend a helping hand to the less fortunate."

As President of the Universal Negro Improvement Assocation, I now declare that it is not my intention or the intention of the society to belabour any race question in this country as some may be inclined to believe and as some envious and wicked minds would care to suggest. The race question must never affect us, we must uphold the equity of the land, irrespective of race under our constitution. The British Constitution is free and liberal, and it dispenses justice to everyman within the state. What concerns us here is the development of our people and country. As a society we realise that the negro people of Jamaica need a great deal of improvement. The bulk of our people are in darkness and are really unfit for good society. To the cultured mind the bulk of our people are contemptible – that is to say, they are entirely outside the pale of cultured appreciation. You know this to be true so we need not get uneasy through prejudice. Go into the country parts of Jamaica and you see there villainy and vice of the worse kind, immorality, obeah, and all kinds of dirty things are part of the avocation of a large percentage of our people and we, the few of cultured tastes, can in no way save the race from injury in a balanced comparison with other people, for the standard of races or of anything else is not arrived at by the few who are always the exceptions, but by the majority. Kingston, and its environs are so infested with the uncouth and vulgar of our people that we of the cultured class feel positively ashamed to move about, and through this state of affairs some of our most representative men even flatter themselves to believe that they are not of us and practically refuse to identify themselves with the people. Well, this society has set itself the task to go among the people and help them up to

A BETTER STATE OF APPRECIATION

among the cultured classes, and raise them to the standard of
civil[iz]ed approval. To do this we must get the co-operation and
sympathy of our white brothers. I know full well that the white
people of this country sympathise with the struggling condition of
their black fellow-citizens and that they would do anything that is
reasonable and in their power to help the people to rise. Whatever
we have achieved from slavery up that is commendable is due to
their broadmindedness and help. The cultured within our fold have
them to thank for all that they have achieved through their open
institutions and philanthropic principles. They have done as much,
and even more than should be expected of them, to advance our
people. What we lack is self-help, and self-reliance, and even with
our culture we lack this. We are always wanting somebody to do
something for us. We depend too much on the large-heartedness of
the individual and we expect too much of the state. As a people, we
are always blaming someone else or the state for the lack of
progress; but I swear it by God that it is the people who have kept
back themselves. My opinion is that we are too envious, malicious
and superficial, and because of this we keep back ourselves and
eventually keep back the country. If we could succeed in producing a
better class of people, less envious, less superficial, more industrious, real, cultured and appreciable, we could then boast of a
country comparable with any other in any part of the world. We do
not want you to envy the rich man and use his riches as an
argument against him. Every rich man has his mission and a duty
to perform; and it is, therefore, good that we have rich men. Every
country of consequence has rich men, and if we were to disgust our
rich men, then the country would go to the dogs. Rich men are the
props of all communities, and if is were not for the rich men of
Jamaica the country would be no fit place to live in, for then villainy
and vice and all kinds of evil would be more rampant. It is the rich
men who provide work for us and help us to live for we have been
unable to do anything for ourselves. Admire your rich men and
[re]spect your superiors and do your best to

RISE ABOVE YOUR PRESENT CONDITION

This is a better lesson than superficial bigotry and inactivity and the
desire to force ourselves up to what we are not. Let us all join hands
to lift the people, without prejudice to any class or colour. To achieve
the ends of a better state among our people, our society desires to

establish an Industrial Farm and Institute on these objects:

1. Providing work for the unemployed.
2. Training our men to a better knowledge and appreciation of agriculture and soil.
3. Teaching our people to be industrious.
4. Providing better and more skilled agricultural workers;
5. Teaching the highest efficiency in the trades,
6. Fitting our young men and women for a better place in the moral and social life of our country.
7. Training our young women to be good and efficient domestics, etc.
8. Providing a good educational training for those who lacked the opportunity in earlier years.
9. And we desire to establish a department for reclaiming and providing ready work for discharging prisoners so as to keep the[m] from returning to crime, namely, praedial larceny, petty thefts, etc.

In a word, our society desires to establish a Tuskegee in Jamaica. These are objects that should commend themselves to every man who loves Jamaica and desires to see the people prosper. Who is against this let him show himself and we shall then say traitor. There is nothing to begrudge in the scheme, for if we are rendered able to achieve these things our country would become the better for our efforts. The better class would have to meet with a better class of peasantry, more intelligent, refined and cultured, the opposite of which they now meet and perforce mix with. The country would then be able to produce a better working class fit for association, controllable and tolerable. I am now appealing to Jamaica at large to help our society to establish this farm and institute. Now is the time for the true friends of the people to show themselves by helping the scheme. We haven't the money to start with so we are about to appeal to the generous people of Jamaica and our friends in America, and we shall be asking you to help us with your penny, shilling or pound to start this institution. Every penny given to this scheme shall be acknowledged in the newspapers, and a statement be given to the people. We are passing through a difficult time, but we can still do something, and I feel sure that our white brothers are going to help us even as they have so willingly done in the past, for they wish us well and they have all along been our dear friends and protectors; and may God bless them in this

THEIR FIGHT FOR LIBERTY

and we still sincerely pray that the day of victory for the Allies be not far off.

Booker T. Washington, America's "great man," has promised to help the society and he has written me this letter:...

Now, friends, now countrymen, let us do something to help the people and country. let us throw individual prejudice aside and help the scheme. I have done my best to bring into existence and keep alive this society that has been doing so much in this community. God alone knows what I have suffered and borne to keep the society, but those who desire to serve the people must be prepared for the criticism of the unjust and uncharitable. It is all well for men to sit by and talk and criticise; all this is cheap; what we want to-day is action backed up with a true manhood. I am not one of the "gassy crew". I am man of action and every word I utter at any time I mean to put into action and you can depend on it. I have given up myself to work in the interest of our people, and I mean to work, work, work, and I leave the rest to God. All of us can help in this effort; those who can't dedicate their lives to the cause, as I have done, can help with money and moral aid, and in some way or the other everybody can do something. I have been helped in my earlier efforts by several of the gentry of this country and I feel sure that they will give us a helping h[a]nd with this scheme. Dear friends, let us serve the people, let us serve Jamaica and God will bless us for our little efforts.

Printed in the *Daily Chronicle,* Thursday, 26 August 1915. Address delivered at UNIA general meeting held Tuesday, 24 August 1915, in the Collegiate Hall.

3. Westindies In The Mirror Of Truth

I have been in America eight months. My mission to this country is to lecture and raise funds to help my organization – the Universal Negro Improvement Association of Jamaica – to establish an industrial and educational institute, to assist in educating the Negro youth of that island. I am also engaged in the study of Negro life in this country.

I must say, at the outset, that the American Negro ought to compliment himself, as well as the early prejudice of the South, for the racial progress made in fifty years, and for the discriminating attitude that had led the race up to the high mark of consciousness preserving it from extinction.

I feel that the Negro who has come in touch with western civilization is characteristically the same, and but for the environment, there would have been no marked difference between those of the scattered race in the western hemisphere. The honest prejudice of the South was sufficiently evident to give the Negro of America the real start – the start with a race consciousness, which I am convinced is responsible for the state of development already reached by the race.

A Fred Douglass or a Booker Washington never would have been heard of in American national life if it were not for the consciousness of the race in having its own leaders. In contrast, the Westindies has produced no Fred Douglass, or Booker Washington, after seventy-eight years of emancipation, simply because the Negro people of that section started out without a race consciousness.

I have travelled a good deal through many countries,and from my observations and study, I unhesitatingly and reservedly say that the American Negro is the peer of all Negroes, the most progressive and the foremost unit in the expansive chain of scattered Ethiopia. Industrially, financially, educationally and socially, the Negroes of both hemispheres have to defer to the American brother, the fellow who has revolutionized history in race development inasmuch as to be able within fifty years to produce men and women out of the immediate bond of slavery, the latchets of whose shoes many a "favoured son and daughter" has been unable to loose.

As I travel through the various cities I have been observing with pleasure the active part played by negro men and women in the commercial and industrial life of the nation. In the cities I have already visited which include New York, Boston, Philadelphia, Pittsburgh, Baltimore, Washington and Chicago, I have seen commercial enterprises owned and managed by Negro people. I have seen Negro banks in Washington and Chicago, stores, cafes, restaurants, theaters and real estate agencies that fill my heart with joy to realize, in positive truth, and not by sentiment, that at one centre of Negrodom, at least, the people of the race have sufficient pride to do things for themselves.

The acme of American Negro enterprise is not yet reached. You have still a far way to go. You want more stores, more banks, and bigger enterprises.I hope that your powerful Negro press and the conscientious element among your leaders will continue to aspire you to achieve; I have detected, during my short stay, that even among you there are leaders who are false, who are mere self-seekers, but on the other hand, I am pleased to find good men, and too, those whose fight for the uplift of the race is one of life and death. I have met some personalities who are not prominently in the limelight for whom I have strong regard as towards their sincerity in the cause of race uplift, and I think more of their people as real disciples working for the good of our race than many of the men whose names have become nationally ad internationally known. In New York, I met John E Bruce, a man for whom I have the strongest regard inasmuch as I have seen in him a true Negro, a man who does not talk simply because he is in a position for which he must say or do something, but who feels honoured to be a member. I can also place in his category Dr R.R. Wright, Jr., Dr. Parks, vice-president of the Baptist Union, and Dr. Triley of the M.E. Church of Philadelphia, the Rev. J.C. Anderson of Quinn Chapel [AME Church] and Mrs Ida Wells-Barnett of Chicago. With men and women of this type, who are conscientious workers, and not mere life service dignitaries, I can quite understand that the time is at hand when the stranger, such as I am, will discover the American Negro firmly and strongly set on the pinnacle of fame.

The Westindian Negro who has had seventy-eight years of emancipation has nothing to compare with your progress. Educationally, he has, in the exception, made a step forward, but generally he is stagnant. I have discovered a lot of "vain bluff" as propagated by the irresponsible type of Westindian Negro who has become resident of this country – bluff to the effect that conditions are better in the Westindies than they are in America. Now let me assure you, honestly and truthfully, that they are nothing of the kind. The Westindies in reality could have been the ideal home of the Negro, but the sleeping Westindian has ignored his chance ever since his emancipation,and today he is at the tail end of all that is worth while in the Westindies. The educated men are immigrating to the United States, Canada and Europe; the labouring element are to be found by the thousands in Central and South America. These people are leaving their homes simply because they haven't pride and courage enough to stay at home and combat the forces that make them exiles. If we had the spirit of self-consciousness and reliance, such as you have in America, we would have been ahead of you, and today the standard of Negro Development in the West would have been higher. We haven't the pluck in the Westindies to agitate for or demand a square deal and the blame can be attributed to no other source than indolence and lack of pride among themselves.

Let not the American negro be misled; he occupies the best position among all Negroes up to the present time, and my advice to him is to keep up his constitutional fight for equity and justice.

The Negroes of the Westindies have been sleeping for sevety-eight years and are still under the spell of Rip Van Winkle. These people want a terrific sensation to awaken them of their racial consciousness. We are throwing away good business opportunities in the beautiful islands of the West. We have no banks of our own, no big stores and commercial undertakings, we depend on others as dealers, while we remain consumers. The file is there open and ready for anyone who has the training and ability to become a pioneer. If enterprising Negro Americans would get a hold of some of the wealthy Negroes of the Westindies and teach them how to trade and to do things in the interest of their people, a great good would be accomplished for the advancement of the race.

The Negro masses in the Westindies want enterprises that will help them to dress as well as the Negroes in the North of the United States; to help them to live in good homes and to provide them with furniture on the installment plan; to insure them in sickness and death and to prevent a pauper's grave.

Printed in the *Champion Magazine* ('A Monthly Survey of Negro Achievement')[1] (January 1917): 167-68. Published in Chicago.

4. Addresses Denouncing W.E.B. Du Bois

In our last issue we gave a synopsis of the meeting of the Universal Negro Improvement Assocation and African Communities League, held at Mother Zion A.M.E. Church on March 25, for the purpose of denouncing the recent reactionary attitude of Dr W.E.B. Du Bois with regard to his opposition to the resolutions which appeared in the *Negro World* of March 1, 1919, and which were presented by Mr Eliezer Cadet to the Peace Conference and also to determine the most effectual means of protecting the Association's elected delegate. In this issue we are prepared to give, as promised, a full report of the speeches delivered. The meeting was attended by fully 3000 Negroes and several white men representing the Department of Justice. The meeting was opened with the singing of the hymn "From Greenland's Icy Mountains,'" after which a very inspiring prayer was offered by the Rev. John S. Wilkins, executive secretary of the association...

The chairman before introducing the next speaker took advantage of the opportunity of explaining his psychological view of the efficient members of the Department of Justice, and hoped that the heads of the Department of Justice were doing their duty in crushing autocracy and establishing universal democracy, so that a little may be able to reach the Southern lands. He then introduced the next speaker, Mr Marcus Garvey, President-General of the Universal Negro Improvement Association and African Communities League.

Mr Marcus Garvey said: "Mr Chairman, Ladies and Gentlemen: on behalf of the Universal Negro Improvement Association and [U].N.I.A. and African Communit[i]es League, this meeting was called. Owing to a cable report sent to us on Monday morning [*24 March*] by our representative, Mr Eliezer Cadet, now in France, representing the interest of 12,000,000 American 10,000,000 Westindian Negroes, and 280,000,000 Africans, for which representation he was elected by 7,000 American, African, Westindian, and South and Central American negroes, at a mass meeting in the Palace Casino on December 1, 1918. The cable tells us that he has published certain articles in the French papers expressing the sufferings of our people and the outrages committed in America, and Dr W.E.B. Du Bois has repudiated his statements by defeating his article in the French paper. (For Mr Eliezer Cadet's Speech in France, and resolutions presented to Peace Conference, read *The Negro World* of March 1, 1919).

Because Mr Cadet presented these aims to the French people and to the Peace Conference and got the hearing and sympathy of the French people, and the Peace Conference, Dr Du Bois, who left this country, and who was never elected by any one except by the capitalistic class, because of the favourable impression of our aims upon the minds of the French people, has come out to attack them in the French papers.

Men and women, I am indeed glad to see how we are assembled here tonight and to hear the acclamations given to the type of new Negroes, who spoke previous to me. These are men ranging in age from eighteen to thirty-two; men who would have died in this bloody war if it had continued another two years. If the war had continued for two weeks longer I would have had to go to France and Flanders to die for the Belgian. According to the law I would have been compelled to go. I know there are going to be more wars within the next twenty-five years, and Negroes will be called upon. But the Negro is prepared to emancipate himself on the continent of Africa. The time has come for the emancipation of all peoples, whether Russians, Germans, Poles or Jews. Already the Egyptians are fighting for their freedom, and it will not be surprising to hear India also striking the blow for complete emancipation. Egypt is now striking, and I pray Almighty God to be on the side of Egypt. What is good for the white man by way of freedom is also good [*for*] the black man by way of freedom. Why should Europe emancipate herself and keep Africa under the heel of oppression. Africa must be for the Africans, and them exclusively. Dr Du Bois desires internationalization of Africa for the white man, the capitalistic class of white men. Cannot these hand-picked leaders see that under the League of Nations certain places will be oppressed by mandatories, and unless the entire constitution of the League of Nations be repealed internationalization will be the control of Africa? France, Belgium and Italy have already realized their positions in Africa, because two millions of blacks have gone back to Africa as soldiers. Italy has already lost her individual nationalistic control which she had prior to the outbreak of war. This Government got Dr Du Bois to go to France so that when he returns and everything is settled they can say, "It i[s] you who asked for these things." Men and women of America, Westindies and Africa. Are you prepared to live in slavery everlasting? "No!" shouted the audience.

A UNIVERSAL MESSAGE

The time has come for us to proclaim our freedom and we must say to the white peoples of the world that the millions of Negroes who fought in the war are now getting ready to emancipate themselves on the continent of Africa. There will be a revolution not in America, but in Africa. I want the members of the Department of Justice to understand that we mean nothing that will keep the Negro from being regarded as a loyal American citizen, but we acknowledge no constitutional law at present exisiting in Africa. You, of the Department of Justice, know that three hundred years ago you left your country, went down into Africa and brought 40,000,000 of us here. You told Queen Elizabeth that your object was to civilize and christianize us and on this pretence she signed the charter to empower you to do so. For two hundred years you enslaved us, and now we are going to use the same civilization and christianity that you brought us out here to get, to make Africa free. In America you acknowledged our civilization when you held us up in the subway for our registration cards (laughter). You acknowledged us in the great war. You recognized our civilization when 2,000,000 of us were sent to fight and die in France and Flanders, while you were here in America. When you called us you told us that we were going to fight for worldwide democracy and since all the other peoples have liberated themselves, we are going to get in line and liberate ourselves also.

We speak tonight, not in the spirit of cowardice, but as men who died in France in 1914-1918, and since we could have died in France we can now die right here. We remember the words of Patrick Henry one hundred and forty-three years ago in the Virginia Legislature, when he was endeavouring to lay the foundation of independence. "I care not what others may say, but as for me, give me liberty or give me death," and now as a new people representing a new sentiment we will say: "We care not what others may say, but for us give us liberty or give us death." If there are to be white kings, white emperors and white czars, there must also be Negro men representing the same dignitaries. The spirit of the age is freedom; the spirit of the age is liberty; the spirit to sanctify by the blood of the martyr, and I feel quite sure that there are no cowards among you men and women in this church tonight.

LIBERTY EXPLOITED AND ROBBED

The object of America, for which George Washington and Patrick

Henry fought 140 years ago, are today cast aside and disregarded. Young men and young women, awake! Be ready for the day when Africa shall declare her independence. And why do I say Africa when you are living in the Westindies and America? Because in these places you will never be safe until you launch your protection internally and externally. The Japanese and Chinese are not lynched in this country because of the fear of retaliation. Behind these men are standing armies and navies to protect them. Such is the case with Frenchmen and Englishmen, but Negroes, representing an undignifed and unorganized nation, are lynched, because they know the best that can be done is to hold a mass meeting. It is truly said that we have no original right in America. If the Poles and Hungarians require a national home with national government – and Australia and Canada are white men countries – then it is requisite for 400,000,000 Negroes to have a national home and a national government, and, as I was asked in England and Scotland and Germany what I was doing there, we will also be able to ask somebody, "What are you doing here?

OBJECTS OF THE U.N.I.A.

Ladies and gentlemen, I want you to realize that the Universal Negro Improvement Association and African Communities League, the organization which I have the honour to represent, is a worldwide movement that is endeavouring to unite the sentiment of our people. Our objective is to declare Africa a vast Negro empire. We can see no right in Belgium's retention of the Congo. We are going to wait until peace is completely restored, and then will we work Belgium out. And when we ask Belgium, "What are you doing there?" America will have nothing to do with it. Under the League of Nations when Africa revolts America will have to call upon Negroes to fight Negroes, therefore the League of Nations must be defeated by every Negro in America, or it will mean that Africa will have to fight the combined nations of the world.

UNANIMITY OF SPIRIT

I thank you, ladies and gentlemen, for the spirit of your responsiveness, which is proof that you disfavour the reactionary activities of Dr Du Bois in France. A few minutes after we received the cable we sent our representative what assistance we had, and told him that in forty-eight hours we would call a meeting to stand by him. And we have done so. This is the spirit of the association. In forty-eight hours, twenty-four hours or twelve hours we will be able, I trust, in some future time to call a meeting of 400,000,000 Negroes all over the world and let them know what we mean by it.

AN ALL-IMPORTANT MESSAGE

We are waiting for the next world war – that racial war which Josephus Daniels, Secretary of the Navy, spoke of thirteen months ago. And we are telling the white people of the world to give Negroes liberty and democracy before it comes. If you do not do it, let me say to you that when the 900,000,000 of yellow and brown peoples of Asia line up against the white ones of Europe and America not a Negro will be found fighting on either side.

We wish to enlighten the sentiment of the 400,000,000 of our people for the next world war. Sixty million Huns outraged civilization for four and a half years, and the other whites were unable to beat them until they called out the American Negroes to assist. And we helped so splendidly that Roberts and Johnson alone were able to bring back twenty captives. This shows exactly the spirit of the Negro. We have made 2,000,000 Napoleons in this war – nay, 2,000,000 Wellingtons – therefore there must be a Waterloo; and I say to you young men; middle-aged and old men, that I can see in you a Napoleon surveying the bridge of Lodi; a Brutus reading in his tent at Phillippi; a Richard Coeur de Lion bearing down upon the armies of Saladin; a Crown Prince storming the forts of Verdun, and a Marshal Joffre marshaling the French artillery in counterattack, winning the day, to the everlasting glory of France. I can see in you women a Florence Nightingale, going among the soldiers of the Crimean battlefield. Nay, a Negro Florence Nightingale going among the black soldiers on the battle plains of Africa; a Joan of Arc leading black men on to victory. This is the spirit of the American Negro; this, I think is the spirit of all Negroes.

Negroes of the Westindies, let me tell you that the Universal Negro Improvement Association will expect you to go back to those islands and teach the doctrine of the association. Let them know that they are lynching and burning black men in the South simply because they are black. We want you to do that because we are starting to organize the Negroes of the world. The people in British Honduras are already starting to organize themselves. There our papers are held up in the post office. But I am going down there for two weeks, and I know they will not be able to stop me from speaking. In Jamaica there are 900,000 black people and 15,000 white ones, who are telling the blacks that there is no difference between black people and white people, and at the same time exploiting and robbing them. They are trying to keep our papers away, and saying they must not be circulated. The British government has paid us a compliment by sending to Africa to know if the Negro World is circulated and what effect it has on the sentiment of the people. I am going to spend six months more here, and the next six months will be to clean up the entire Westindian islands.

This is an age in which we must stand up for our constitutional rights[.] Let your brothers and sisters in the Westindies know that the white man has no privilege, pre-eminence or monopoly over them. I want you to understand clearly that I am not telling you to do anything unconstitutionally.

There are several reasons why we are holding this meeting in the church. We are here because God has always been with the Negro and the Negro with God. We are here because we want the blessing of God. At the crucifixion, white men got hold of Christ, beat him and mocked him but, unlike these, Simon, the Cyrenean, a Negro, took his cross and carried it. Jesus, whom we helped, is now in heaven. If man can be grateful, we know the Divine is much more grateful. When the Divine was in trouble we helped Him, and now that we are in trouble we know that he will help us.

Ladies and gentlemen, I am now going to appeal to you to give as liberally as possible to this worthy cause. Your help is required to fight this reactionary leader. At the Palace Casino you gave $220 to fight your noble cause. It will take $780 to fight it and bring your representative back.

M. Cadet's article is already disputed by Dr Du Bois in the French papers, so therefore give as liberally as you can.["]

IMPORTANT RESOLUTION

The chairman upon calling upon W.H. Domingo to move the resolution decided upon to be cabled to the French press, he said: "In rising to move this resolution I desire to preface it. I have favoured, honoured and respected for many years the person against whom this resolution is directed, but in view of the fact that he changed his face and wrote a certain editorial called "Clothed Faces," I am compelled to dishonour and disfavour him."...

A.P. Randolph: "I must felicitate both you and myself of seconding this resolution, which is calculated to demonstrate to the world that we are a people here." The resolution was again read, this time by the chairman and was unanimously carried with acclamations...

The meeting came to a close at 11.30 p.m., followed by the singing of "Onward, Christian Soldiers."

[Printed in the *Negro World,* Saturday, 5 April 1919]

5. Editorial Letter by Marcus Garvey

Fellowmen of the Negro Race,

Greeting: Once more the white man has outraged American Civilization and dragged the fair name of the republic before the Court of Civilized Justice.

Another riot has visited the country and Omaha, Nebraska, has placed her name upon the map of mob violence, so it can be seen that the mob spirit is spreading all over, going from South to East, to mid-West and then to the West.

Mobs of white men all over the world will continue to lynch and burn Negroes so long as we remain divided among ourselves. The very moment all the Negroes of this and other countries start to stand together, that very time will see the white man standing in fear of the Negro race even as he stands in fear of the yellow race of Japan today.

The Negro must now organize all over the world, 400,000,000 strong, to adminster to our oppressors their Waterloo.

No mercy, no respect, no justice will be shown the Negro until he forces all other men to respect him. There have been many riots in the United States and England recently, and immediately following the war of democracy, there will be many more as coming from the white man. Therefore, the best thing the Negro of all countries can do is to prepare to match fire with hell fire. No African is going to allow the Caucasian to trample eternally upon his rights. We have allowed it for 500 years and we have now struck.

Fellowmen of the World, I here beg of you to prepare, for a great day is coming – the day of the war of the races, when Asia will lead out to defeat Europe[,] and Europe and the white man will again call upon the Negro to save them as we have often done.

The New Negro has fought the last battle for the white man, and he is now getting ready to fight for the redemption of Africa. With mob laws and lynching bees fresh in our memories, we shall turn a deaf ear to the white man when Asia administers to him his final "licking," and place and keep him where he belongs.

If the white men were wise, they would have treated Negroes differently, but to our astonishment they are playing the part of the dog by biting the hand that feeds. If it were not for the Negro, the white man would have been lost long ago. The black man has saved him and the only thanks we get today is mob law.

Let every Negro all over the world prepare for the new emancipation. The Fatherland, Africa, has been kept by God Almighty for the Negro to redeem, and we, young men and women of the race, have pledged ourselves to plant the flag of freedom and of Empire.

Our forces of industry, commerce, science, art, literature and war must be marshalled when Asia or Europe strikes the blow of a second world war. Black men shall die then and black women shall succor our men, but in the end there shall be a crowning victory for the soldiers of Ethiopia on the African battlefield.

And now let me remind all of you, fellowmen, to do your duty to the Black Star Line Steamship Corporation, of 56 West 135th Street, New York City, United States of America. This corporation is endeavouring to float a line of steamships to handle the Negro trade of the world, to run a line of steamships between America, Canada, South and Central America, the Westindies and Africa, to link up the Negro peoples of the world in trade and commerce. The shares are now going at $5.00 each, and I now ask you to buy as many shares as you can and make money while the opportunity presents itself. You can buy from one to two hundred shares right now.

Send in today and buy 5, 10, 20, 40, 100 or 200 shares. Write to The Black Star Line Steamship Corporation, 56 West 135th Street, New York, N.Y. U.S.A. With very best wishes, Yours fraternally, Marcus Garvey

Printed in *Negro World,* 11 October 1919; reprinted in the *Emancipator,* 27 March 1920.

6. Speech by Marcus Garvey

...Last night the People's Church, corner of Fifteenth and Christian Street, was the scene of wild enthusiasm, when the Honourable Marcus Garvey, president-general of the Universal Negro Improvement Association and president of the Black Star Line Steamship Corporation, appeared to speak. Mr Garvey opened a campaign here last Sunday which opening was very successful. Thousands jammed the church, and thousands were turned away unable to get admittance.

...MR GARVEY'S SPEECH

Mr President, Lady President, Ladies and Gentlemen: Once more it is my pleasure to be with you. That you have turned out in such large numbers tonight proves beyond the shadow of a doubt that you good people of the race in Philadelphia are very much alive to the principles, to the aims, to the objects of the greatest movement among Negroes in the world today – the Universal Negro Improvement Association and African Communities League. It is the greatest movement in the world, because it is the only movement today that is causing the white man to tremble in his shoes. (Cheers.) The white man has had the policies of our great men or the great leaders of the past. They have had the policies of Booker Washington, they have had the policies of the other great leaders of this country, of the Westindies and of Africa, but out of these policies nothing ever came to the Negro, and the white man was satisfied. They have buried our great leader in America, Booker Washington, and yet we have achieved nothing by way of our own initiative. They have buried the great leaders of the Negro race of other countries, and yet we have achieved nothing, except in the Republic of Haiti, where one Negro repelled them and established an independent republic. I speak of Haiti. They did not like Toussaint L'O[u]verture because he had initiative. They lied to him, they deceived him, and when he had just a little faith still in them they destroyed that faith. They made a prisoner of him, took him to France, and there he died. Thank God, as Toussaint L'Ourverture in his time was able to inspire the other men of his country to carry on the work until Haiti was made a free country, so today we have inspired not one, not two, but hundreds of thousands to carry out the work even if they imprison one or kill one.

It is for me to say to you faithful members and followers of the

Universal Negro Improvement Association in Philadelphia that the movement that you are in is a movement that is causing not merely the individual white man, but governments to be living in fear as touching the outcome of the Negro peoples of the world through their determination in the Universal Negro Improvement Association.

THOUSANDS JAMMED HALL

Last night, after I was through addressing my people in New York, about 5,000 of them jammed themselves into Liberty Hall, overtaxing the capacity of that building, and we had to turn away about 10,000, and there were fully 3,000 around the building, trying to get in last night. The biggest meeting we ever had in Harlem was last night, when we had fully between twenty and thirty thousand Negroes trying to get into Liberty Hall. After I was through addressing the good people there, one of the members brought me a letter he had received from his friend in Panama. They did not know that the Universal Negro Improvement Association has secret service men all over the world now, and the letter said that just two hours before he read a cable which was sent by the Canal Commission in Panama beseeching Washington not to give a passport to Marcus Garvey to visit Panama, because if he landed there, there would be trouble for the white man there. Now, you know who are the people who are controlling the Panama Canal under this administration. They are Southern white men. The chicken is going home to roost. We told those Southern crackers that one day the Negro would get even with them. You see how cowardly they are. Now, I am quite away in New York and they are begging the people here not to let me get out of New York to go there. But to show you how puzzled they are: My District Attorney friend in New York has been trying for many months to get me expelled from the country. Some want me to go and some don't want me to go. What must I do? To my mind, it is a question of being between hell and the powder house. (Laughter).

ANCIENT FOE PUZZLED

Now, that is what we can compliment ourselves for today. We have our foe, our ancient foe, puzzled. He does not know what to do with the New Negro; but the New Negro knows what to do with himself. And the thing that we are going to do is to blast a way to complete independence and to that democracy which they denied us even after we left the battlefields of France and Flanders. We, the New Negroes, say there is no turning back for us now. There is nothing else but a going forward, and if they squeal in America or anywhere else we are going forward. Why, we are not organized as four hundred millions yet, and they are so scared. Now, what will happen in the next five years when the entire four hundred millions will have been organized? All the lynching in the South will be a thing of the past. We are determined in this association to bring the white man to his senses. We are not going to fight and kill anybody because he has more than we have. But if there is anybody taking advantage of the Negro, whether he be white, red or blue, we are going to organize to stop him. We believe that white men have as much right to live as yellow men; we believe that yellow men have as much right to live as red men; we believe that red men have as much right to live as black men, and we believe that black men have as much right to live as all men. Therefore, if any race of mankind says that the other race must die, it is time for that race that is dying to organize to prevent themselves from dying. And as for me, the sweetest life in the world to me is the life of my race. I cannot change my race overnight. You cannot change your race overnight. We have not been able to change our race for three hundred years. No one can change our race overnight. God created us what we are and we are going to remain what we are until Gabriel blows his horn.

Therefore we are of the Negro race and we are suffering simply because we are of the Negro race, and since we are four hundr[e]d million strong, it is for us to organize that strong to protect our race. And I want you young men, you middle aged men and you old men of the race and women also to realize that this is the age of action – action on the part of each and every individual of every race. If there is a white man who does not love the white race, to his race he is an outcast; if there is a yellow man that does not love his race, to the yellow race he is an outcast; if there is a Negro who does not love the black race, to his race such a Negro is an outcast and should be trampled to death.

FARCE OF BROTHERHOOD

We have lived upon the farce of brotherhood for hundreds of years, and if there is anybody who has suffered from that farce it is the Negro. The white man goes forth with the Bible and tells us that we are all brothers, but it is against the world to believe, against all humanity to believe, that really there is but one brotherhood. And if there are six brothers in any family, at least those six brothers from natural tie ought to be honest in their dealings with each other to the extent of not seeing any of the six starve. If one has not a job, naturally the others would see to it that the one that is out of a job gets something to eat and a place to sleep so as to prevent him from starving and dying. This is brotherhood. Now there is one brother with all the wealth; he has more than he wants, and there is the other brother. What is he is doing to the other brother? He is murdering the other brother. He is lynching the other brother, and still they are brothers. Now, if I have any brother in my family who has no better love for me than to starve me, to whip me and to burn me, I say, brother, I do not want your relationship at all. To hell with it.

No, sir, I strike against the idea of brotherhood as coming from that man. I believe in the brotherhood of man. I believe in the fatherhood of God, but as man sinned and lost his purpose ever since the fall of Adam and Eve, I also realize that man has lost his closest connection, his closest tie, with his God. And since man is human, since man has lost his instinct divine, I am not going to trust man. From the attitude of man, from the action of man today, I can see that every one is looking out for himself where the question of race comes in. The white race is looking out for the white race; the yellow race is looking out for the yellow race or Asiatic race. The time has come when the Negro should look out for himself and let the others look out for themselves. This is the new doctrine today. It is the doctrine of Europe. Europe is looking out for the white man. It is the doctrine of Asia. Asia is looking out for the yellow man. So should Africa look out for the black man, the Negro. And since they (the whites) have divided up Africa, having a part in America, a part in Canada, a part in the Westindies, a part in Central America, a part in South America, and a part remaining in Africa, we are saying that the time has come that there should be a united Africa. And before a united Africa comes, Ethiopia, as scattered as she is, must stretch forth her hands unto God.

TIME TO HELP SELF

Tonight the Universal Negro Improvement Association is endeavouring to teach Negroes that the time has come for them to help themselves. We have helped the white man in this Western Hemisphere for over three hundred years until he has become so almighty that he respects not even God himself. The white man believes that there is only one God, and that is the white man. We have a different idea about God. We believe that there is but one God, and he is in a place called heaven. There is a heaven, we believe, and a God presides over that heaven, and as far as the Negro is concerned that God is the only being in the world whom we respect. We believe with Theodore Roosevelt, "FEAR GOD AND

KNOW NO OTHER FEAR." And if every Negro in Philadelphia could just get that one thought into his or her mind, to fear God and him alone and let the world take care of itself, the better it would be for each and every one.

WHITE MAN'S IMPERIAL MAJESTY

The white man comes before you in his imperial and majestic pomp and tries to impress upon you the idea that he is your superior. Who made him your superior? You stick his face with a pin and blood runs out. You stick the black man's face with a pin and blood runs out. Starve the white man and he dies. Starve the black man and he dies. What difference is there, therefore, in black and white. If you stick the white man, blood come[s] out. If you starve the white man he dies. The same applies to the black man. They said the white man was the superior being and the black man was the inferior being. That is the old time notion, but today the world knows that all men were created equal. We were created equal and were put into this world to possess equal rights and equal privileges, and the time has come for the black man to get his share. The white man has got his share and more than his share for thousands of years, and we are calling upon him now to give up that which is not his, so that we can have ours. Some of them will be wise enough and sensible enough to give up what is not is theirs to save confusion. You know when a man takes what is not his, the one from whom he took that thing is going to take him to court so as to recover his loss. Now, the Negro is going to take somebody to a court of law one day. This court is not going to be presided over by the white man. It is the court to be presided over and decided by the sword. Yes; the sword will decide to whom belongs the right.

AFRICA TO CALL FOR A JUDGMENT

And I want you men of Africa, you men of the Negro race, to prepare for the day when Africa will call for a judgement. Africa is preparing to call for a judgment, and that judgment we must have, and it will be a judgment in favour of four hundred million oppressed people. And the marshal who will carry out the authority of the court will be the new Toussaint L'Ouverture with the sword and the banner of the new African Republic. You black men of Philadelphia sit here tonight as jurors in the case where judgment is to be given in favour of the Negro, and I am now asking you jurymen: Gentlemen of the jury, what is your verdict? Cries of: "Africa must be free!" Now, if Africa is to be free, it means, therefore, that Philadelphia has given her verdict as we have in New York. It is now for the judge to give his finding. The judge will give his finding after all the jurors of the Negro race, four hundred million, will have given their verdict. And then after the judge gives his finding he will have to find a marshal to serve the writ, who will require the New Negro to help him to serve this writ, because the man to whom this writ is to be served is of a desperate character, because he prefers to shed blood and take lives before he will give up what is not his. You have to spill blood in Africa before you get what is belonging to you.

A NEGRO GOVERNMENT

Therefore, you will realize that the Universal Negro Improvement Association is no joke. It is as serious a movement as the movement of the Irish today to have a free Ireland; as the determination of the Jew to recover Palestine. The Negro peoples of the world should be so determined to reclaim Africa and found a government there, so that if any black man in any part of the world is abused we can call the mighty power of Africa to come to our aid. Men, a Negro government we had once, and a Negro government we must have again. Tell me that I must live everlastingly under the domination of a white man, that I must bequeath to my children white overlordship, then I say, let me die now, Almighty God. If there is no better future in the world for me than to be the slave of a white man, I say, take the life you gave me. I do not want it. You would not be my God if you created me to be a slave to other men; but you are my God and will continue to be my God if you created me an equal of all men.

LIFE GIVEN FOR A PURPOSE

Men, I want you to realize that the life you live was given you for a purpose; not for the purpose of being a slave, not for the purpose of being a serf, but for the purpose of being a man, and for that purpose you must live, or it is better you die.

THE NEGRO WILL DIE ECONOMICALLY

Now I want to come to the practical, common sense side of this question. We have started an agitation all over the world. It is the agitation of self-reliance wherein the Negro must do for himself. I want you to understand that if you do not get behind this agitation and back it up morally and financially you are only flirting with your own downfall, because the world in which we live is today more serious than it ever was. White and yellow men have become more selfish today than they were before causing the terrible war, the terrible conflict, of 1914 to 1918. They destroyed all that they spent years and years to build and all the time and energy they gave us counted for nought because of the destruction. They have, therefore, lost their sympathies for other men. They have lost their sympathies for other races and have settled down to see nothing else but their own interest until they will have succeeded in rebuilding themselves. During this selfish, soulless age it falls to the province of the Negro to take the initiative and do for himself; otherwise he is going to die. He is going to d[ie,] as I stand on this platform tonight[,] economically in America; he is going to die economically under the yoke of Britain, of France and of Germany. He is going to die in the next one hundred years if he does not start out now to do for himself.

DEAR AMERICA FOR WHITE MEN

I want you to realize that this dear America, the greatest democracy in the world for white men, the greatest republic in the world for white men, that this America is becoming more prejudiced every day against the Negro. Month by month they are lynching more Negroes than they ever did before; month by month more riots are going on in the industrial sections of this country than ever before. This is an indication of the spirit of the people that are living today. It is the spirit that will be bequeathed to their children and to the unborn posterity of the white race. If you think that the white man is going to be more liberal to Negroes than they are at present, you are making a big mistake. Every succeeding generation of the white race is getting more prejudiced against the Negro. It is time, therefore, for the Negro to look our for the future for himself.

FOUR HUNDRED MILLION WHITES

We have in America ninety million white fellow citizens, and they are lynching us by the dozen every day. In the next one hundred years you are going to have four hundred million people (white) in America. Now, if they are lynching twelve a day with their ninety millions, how many are they going to lynch when they are four hundred millions. I want you to figure this out for yourselves. And it is because our old time leaders failed to see this that we of the Universal Negro Improvement Association say that the old time leadership must go.

NEGROES FLIRTING WITH THEIR GRAVES

Again I want you to understand that economically we are flirting with our graves if we do not start to make ourselves economically independent. This war brought about new conditions in America and all over the world. America sent hundreds of thousands of coloured soldiers to fight the white man's battles, during which time she opened the doors of industry to millions of white American men and women and created a new problem in the industrial market. And now the war is over and those millions who took the places of the soldiers who have returned home say: "We are not going to give up our jobs. We are going to remain in the industrial life of the world.["] This makes it difficult for returned soldiers to get work now. There will be sufficient jobs now for returned soldiers and for white men, because abnormal conditions are still in existence, but in the next two years these abnormal conditions will pass away and the industries will not be opened up for so long. It means that millions are going to starve. Do you think the white industrial captains are going to allow the white men and the white women to starve and give you bread? To the white man blood is thicker than water.

Therefore, in the next two years there is going to be an industrial boomerang in this country, and if the Negroes do not organize now to open up economic and industrial opportunities for themselves there will be starvation among all Negroes. It is because we want to save the situation when this good time shall have passed by and the white man calls you, "My dear John, I haven't any job for you today," and you can leave the white man's job as porter and go into the Negro factory as a clerk, you can leave the white man's kitchen and go into your home as the wife of a big Negro banker or a corporation manager.

THE BLACK STAR LINE

That is why we want the Black Star Line so as to launch out to the Negro peoples of the world, and today the richest people of the world are the Negro people of Africa. Their minerals, their diamonds, their gold and their silver and their iron have built up the great English, French, German and Belgian Empires. Men, how long are we going to allow those parasites to suck the blood out of our children? How long? I answer for those who are active members of the Universal Negro Improvement Association and African Communities League, "Not one day longer." No parasite shall continue to feed off my body, because I want to have a healthy body. I have not sufficient blood to give to any parasite, because when I get sick I will need every drop of my blood to sustain me until I am well, so while I am well I will have to take off that parasite and throw it away. The time has come for the Negro to exert his energy to the utmost to do. Men and women of Philadelphia, the question is now for you to decide. Are you ready tonight or are you going to wait for two years more to be ready. The answer is, "You must be ready now[.]" Thank God, there are millions of us who are ready already, and when the Black Star Line sails out, by the demonstration of the Black Star Line spontaneously and simultanously, millions will become [wealthy?].

SOME BAD NEGROES

Some bad Negroes, and I understand some are in Philadelphia, say there will be no Black Star Line. I am only sorry that I have not the time to waste or the strength or energy to give away that when I come against those bad Negroes to just get a big stick and give them a good walloping, because such Negroes are not entitled to courteous treatment. I want you active members not to waste time with such Negroes, but to put them down. Mark them well, because those are the same guys who, after you have achieved through your sacrifice, will go around and say: "We did it; we did it." The so-called big Negroes are the ones who have kept back the race. Some of them are doctors and lawyers and other professionals. They feel they are not belonging to the other class of Negroes. Those are the people who have done nothing to help the race because they sell out the race. This Black Star Line we are putting forward is an industrial proposition, and we are putting this proposition forward not by the big Negroes, but by the small Negroes. The first ship of the Black Star Line that we are to float on the 31st of this month will be owned not by the big Negroes, but by the small Negroes, and on that day we are going to say to the big Negroes, "Now, who are the big Negroes;" We who have made the Black Star Line possible are the big Negroes. In New York we have discarded that kind of big Negroes. If they want to be big, they have to come right in line with other Negroes and show how big they are. We are not going to take it for granted that you are big. You have to show how big you are, not by the amount of money that you have, not by the automobile that you can afford to run, but by your sacrifice for your race. The sacrifice that you are prepared to make, that is how we are going to make men big. The so-called big Negro tells you that he is an aristocratic Negro; he is a gentleman. I want to know where the Negro aristocrat came from. A little more than fifty years ago Abraham Lincoln took up the pen and liberated four million Negroes. He did not say to any particular one, "You are a big Negro," or "You are an aristocrat," or "You are inferior." Victoria, eighty-two or eighty-three years ago, took up the pen and liberated a few million Negroes in the Westindies, but she did not classify them. All of us got our emancipation on equal terms, and it is for those who have the noblest blood, feeling and sentiment towards humanity to come out and do service so as to distinguish ourselves from the rest. Have they done it? Outside of Booker Washington and Frederick Douglass, there is not another aristocratic Negro in America. Douglass and Washington are the only two Negroes in this country who went out and did service so as to make themselves singular among the Negroes of America. It was not a matter of money that made these two men big Negroes. It was nobility of soul, of spirit, to do service to suffering humanity, and that made them different from the rest of the people. That made them aristocrats among their own. But these fat headed, big belly politicians who have robbed the people in their votes at the polls for a few dollars go among the people and say: "We are the aristocrats; we are the big Negroes." Indeed, I refuse to respect any such big Negroes. Show me the Negro of Booker Washington's stamp, show me the Negro of Frederick Douglass' stamp, and I will say, "There go the aristocratic Negroes of the race!"

NOBILITY THROUGH SERVICE

Men become noble through service. Therefore, if any Negro wants to call himself an aristocrat, a nobleman, before he will get that respect from me he will have to do some service to the Negro race. So you lawyers, you doctors and you politicians who think you are big Negroes we want to tell you that you are nothing for us, of the Universal Negro Improvement Association and African Communities League. You have to do service, and the time will come when we will give you a chance, when we will give you the opportunity to do service, because we are going to want hundreds of you professional men to lead the Negro forces on to VICTORY.

So tonight I want you men and women to understand that there is a chance for every one of you tonight to do service to your race, to humanity, before I leave this building for New York, and that is to help to launch on the 31st of this month the first ship of the Black Star Line. I want you all to buy as many shares as you can. If you can buy twenty, buy them; if you can buy fifteen, buy them; if you can buy ten, buy them. Buy as many as you possibly can, so as to render service to yourselves, service to your race, service to humanity.

Printed in *Negro World,* 1 November 1919.

7. Report of the UNIA Meeting

...Last night the First Baptist Church of this city was the scene of wildest enthusiasm when the Hon. Marcus Garvey and party entered the building for the purpose of starting a campaign for sales of stocks in the Black Star Line Steamship Corporation of which Mr Garvey is President. The party consisted of Mrs Estelle Matthews, President of the Ladies' Division of the Philadelphia branch of the Universal Negro Improvement Association; Miss Amy Ashwood, General Secretary of the Ladies' Division of the New York branch of the Universal Negro Improvement Association; Mr Elie Garcia, General Secretary of Philadelphia Division of the Universal Negro Improvement Association and Mr Robert Cross, official stenographer of the Black Star Line Steamship Corporation and reporter of *The Negro World*.

Seated on the platform were Hon. Marcus Garvey, Mr R.H. Taylor, President of the local division of the Universal Negro Improvement Association; Mrs Estelle Matthews, Rev. Dr Taylor and others. Mr R.H. Taylor presided, and at the close of his opening remarks he introduced Dr Taylor, the Treasurer of the local division of the Universal Negro Improvement Association, who gave a stirring address, in which he said that this organization is going to stand as long as God lives. In the last great war, he said, the white men told the coloured ministers of the Gospel to teach their people patriotism for America so that all our men may go to France and fight and die for the white man's democracy, and the coloured parsons were very active in so doing. He said that our coloured men were deceived by the coloured parsons, for they told us that we were also going to enjoy that democracy and liberty after we returned from the war. But now that we have returned, instead of getting the liberty and democracy for which we fought and died in France and Flanders, he said, we are being lynched and burned more than ever. Mr Taylor said that if the preachers cannot lead him temporally they cannot lead him spiritually. He said that many of our coloured organizations have broken down because they had the wrong leaders, leaders who were chosen by [the] white man. But he was glad to say that tonight we have a leader that a white man did not put before us. We have a leader, he said, that God sent to us. He exhorted us to stand by this leader, the Hon. Marcus Garvey, and hold up his arms and victory shall be ours.

MRS MATTHEWS' ADDRESS

Most Honourable President-General, Ladies and Gentlemen – I assure you it affords me great pleasure at this most opportune time to come to you this evening with a message. I come to you from the City of Brotherly Love and from the Philadelphia Division of the Universal Negro Improvement Association. But as I come to you in these serious times, when right is on the scaffold and wrong is on the throne, when we can almost smell the smoke of our lynched brothers and sisters, when we can hear the cries of our brothers and sisters for mercy in Georgia and other states, up to now we have not been able to do anything but pity them. We can even hear the cries of millions of our unborn children for mercy, and up until this present time we have not made the way clear for them. Friends, we are living in a serious age, and the thought comes to me tonight that the hour has struck for Negro manhood and womanhood for action.

THREE MILLION GALLONS OF WHISKEY IN AFRICA

For five hundred years the Anglo-Saxon, the white man, the worst enemy that the Negro ever had, has been acting for us. He has acted for our brothers and sisters in Africa. One writer says in the course of four short years the white men of England and America sent three million gallons of whiskey to help civilize our black brothers when they acted for them, and that is why we are divided today. We have allowed the white man, the white woman, to act for us, and they have acted along every line and we are dismembered, disorganized, confused and puzzled until we do not know where to go or what to do. We do not know whom to follow. They have acted for us and told us we could not organize; we could not think for ourseves; we could not fight for ourselves.

We have proven him a liar in that line. (Cheers). We have proven that we can fight him when he runs, and we are now going to fight for ourselves. (Cheers.)

We have allowed him to act for us in making us pay more taxes for our back alley house and unsanitary conditions of our streets in our large cities. We have allowed the white man to act for us, and there we have sent our boys and girls to build up those disreputable places, while the white was out in the suburbs in mansions and did not come near us. We have allowed him to act for us in doing everything.

NEGROES TOLD NOT TO ORGANIZE

The white man has told you not to organize because you cannot get any leader and that your leaders have betrayed you, and we have allowed them to lead us, and they have been leading us right back into slavery. They have led us so much that they have been leading us right back into slavery. They have led us so much that the majority of Negroes like white men and they mistrust their own. All the devilry we have had among ourselves was caused by the drops of white blood we had in us.

I beg you men and women of my race, tonight, if I can do any good, I want to make you think. No race can rise except they begin to think. We must think for ourselves and stop letting the white man think for us. How can we think for ourselves? The cause is here, the man is here, the problem is before you. We have heard him talk time and again. Some of us are sta[u]nch members; others are not. But as the great leader, the Hon. Marcus Garvey, talks tonight, I want you to sink every word into your hearts.

MR GARVEY'S ADDRESS

Mr President, Offices and members of the Newport News Division of the Universal Negro Improvement Association – Indeed, it is a pleasure to be with you. From the first time I visited your city I became impressed with your earnestness. Ever since I came here and went away an impression, an indelible impression, was made on me relative to your earnestness in the great onward and upward movement engineered under the leadership of the Universal Negro Improvement Association.

Since I visited you last the Universal Negro Improvement Association has grown financially and otherwise, numerically, to the extent that tonight, this very hour the Universal Negro Improvement Association is regarded as the strongest Negro movement in the world. (Cheers.) We have been able to force entry into every civilized country where Negroes live, and tonight the colours that you and I are wearing in Newport News are being worn by Negroes all over the world.

U.N.I.A. SERIOUS MOVEMENT

As I have told you in many addresses before, the Universal Negro Improvement Association is a very serious movement. We are out for serious business. We are out for the capturing of liberty and democracy. (Cheers.) Liberty is not yet captured, therefore we are still fighting. We are in a very great war, a great conflict, and we will never get liberty, we will never capture democracy, until we, like all the other peoples who have won liberty and democracy, shed our sacred blood. This liberty, this democracy, for which we Negroes of the world are hoping, is a thing that has caused blood as a sacrifice by every people who possess it today.

THE DEFEAT OF GERMANY

The white man of America who possesses his liberty and his democracy won it through the sacrifice of those thousands of soldiers who fought and fell under the leadership of George Washington. The French people, who are enjoying their liberty and their democracy today, are enjoying it because thousands of Frenchmen fought, bled and died to make France safe. That America, England and France have had the peace with the world and with themselves is simply through the fact that they have defeated Germany and won for themselves liberty and democracy.

LIBERTY AND DEMOCRACY EXPENSIVE

Therefore, you will realize that liberty and democracy are very expensive things, and you have to give life for it. And if we Negroes think we can get all these things without the shedding of blood for them we are making a dreadful mistake. You are not going to get anything unless you organize to fight for it. There are some things you can fight for constitutionally, such as your political rights, your civic rights, but to get liberty you have to shed some blood for it. And that is what the Universal Negro Improvement Association is preparing your minds for – to shed some blood so as to make your race a free and independent race. That blood we are not going to shed in Newport News, that blood we are not going to shed in America, because America will not be big enough to hold the Negro when the Negro gets ready. But that blood we are preparing to shed one day on the African battlefield, because it is the determination of the New Negro to re-possess himself of that country that God gave his forefathers. Africa is the richest continent in the world; it is the country that has given civilization to mankind and has made the white man what he is.

WHAT THE WHITE MAN OWES THE NEGRO

After the white man is through abusing the Negro, when he gets back his sober senses, he will realize that he owes all he possesses today to the Negro. The Negro gave him science and art and literature and everything that is dear to him today, and the white man has kept them for thousands of years, and he has taken advantage of the world. He has even gone out of his way to reduce the African that gave him his civilization and kept him as a slave for two hundred and fifty years. But we feel that the time has come when we must take hold of that civilization that we once held. The hour has struck for the Negro to be once more a power in the world, and not all the white men in the world will be able to hold the Negro from becoming a power in the next century. Not even the powers of hell will be able to stop the Negro in his onward and upward movement. With Jesus as our standard bearer the Negro will march to victory.

THE NEGRO RULES

There will be no democracy in the world until the Negro rules. We have given the white man a chance for thousands of years to show his feeling towards his fellow men. And what has he done up to this twentieth century? He has murdered man; he has massacred man; he has deprived man of his rights even as God gave to man. The white man has shown himself an unfit subject to rule. Therefore he has to step off the stage of action.

I believe it is Shakespeare who said:

The Quality of mercy is not strained,
It droppeth like the gentle rain from heaven
Upon the place beneath;
It is twice blessed;
It blesseth him that gives and him that takes."

Has the white man any mercy? Not before the black man returns to power will there be any mercy in the world. The Negro has been the saviour of all that has been good for mankind.

But the future portends great things. It portends a leadership of Negroes that will draw man nearer to his God, because in the Negroes' rule there will be mercy, love and charity to all.

MAN CREATED FOR A PURPOSE

I want you coloured men and women in Newport News to realize that you form a great part in this creation, for God has created you for a purpose; that purpose you have to keep in view; that purpose you must live. God said throught the Psalmist that Ethiopia shall stretch forth her hands unto him and that princes shall come out of Ethiopia. I believe fervently that the hour has come for Ethiopia to stretch forth her hands unto God, and as we are stretching forth our hands unto God in New York, in Pennsylvania, in the Westindies, in Central America and in Africa and throughout the world I trust that you in Newport News are stretching forth your hands unto God.

ENDLESS CHAIN OF NEGROES

There is an endless chain of Negroes all over the world, and wherever Negroes are to be found this day they are suffering from the brutality of the white man, and because Negroes are suffering all over the world we feel that the time has come for the four hundred millions of us scattered all over the world to link up our sentiment for one common purpose – to obtain liberty and demoracy.

AFRICA MUST BE RESTORED

I want you to understand that you have an association that is one of the greatest movements in the world. The New Negro, backed up by the Universal Negro Improvement Association, is determined to restore Africa to the world, and you scattered children of Africa in Newport News, you children of Ethiopia, I want you to understand that the call is now made to you. What are you going to do? Are you going to remain to yourselves in Newport News and die? Or are you going to link up your strength, morally and financially, with the other Negroes of the world and let us all fight one battle unto victory? If you are prepared to do the latter, the battle is nearly won, because we of the Universal Negro Improvement Association intend within the next twelve months to roll up a sentiment in the United States of America that will be backed up by fifteen million black folks, so that when in the future you touch one Negro in Newport News you shall have touched fifteen million Negroes of the country. And within the next twenty-four months we intend to roll up an organization of nearly four hundred million people, so that when you touch any Negro in Newport News you touch four hundred million of Negroes all over the world at the same time.

LIBERTY OR DEATH

It falls to the province of every black man and every black woman to be a member of the Universal Negro Improvement Association, because there is but one purpose before us, which is the purpose of liberty – that liberty that Patrick Henry spoke about in the legislature of Virginia over one hundred and forty years ago. We New Negroes of America declare that we desire liberty or we will take death. (Cheers.) They called us out but a few months ago to fight three thousand miles away in Europe to save civilization, to give liberty and democracy to the other peoples of the world. And we fought so splendidly, and after we died, after we gave up our blood, and some of us survived and returned to our respective countries, in America, in the Westindies, in Central America and in Africa, they told us, as they told us in the past, that this country is the white man's country. What is it but menial opportunities for you where you live in contact with white men? Because they have told us that in America, because they have told us that in France, because they have told us under the government of Great Britain that our opportunities are limited when we come in contact with white men, we say the war is not over yet. The war must go on; only that the war is not going on in France and Flanders, but the war will go on in the African plains, there to decide once and for all in the very near future whether black men are to be serfs and slaves or black men are to be free men.

BLACK MEN ARE GOING TO BE FREE

We have decreed that black men are going to be free as white men are free or as yellow men are free. We have declared that if there is to be a British Empire, if there is to be a German Empire, if there is to be a Japanese Empire, if there is to be a French Republic and if there is to be an American Republic, then there must be a black republic of Africa. (Cheers.)

THE WHITE MAN HID THE BOOK FROM THE NEGRO

The New Negro has given up the idea of white leadership. The white man cannot lead the Negro any longer any more. He was able through our ignorance to lead us for over three hundred years since he took us from Africa, but the New Negro has learned enough now. When the white man took the black man from Africa he took him under a camouflage. He said to the Queen of England that he was taking the black man from Africa for the purpose of civilizing and Christianizing him. But that was not his purpose. The white man's purpose for taking the Negro from his native land was to make a slave of him, to have free labour. Some of us were brought to the Southern States of this country, some of our brothers and sisters were taken to Central America and others were taken to the Westindian islands, and we laboured under the bonds of slavery for 250 years. The white man never schooled us for the 250 years. He hid the book from us, even the very Bible, and never taught the Negro anything.

THE NEGRO MADE A RUSH FOR THE BOOK

But God moves in a mysterious way, and he brought about Lincoln and Victoria, and he said, "You must let those people free," and they did let us free. As soon as we were freed we made a rush to get the book, and we did get the book. We got the Bible first, and we began to sing songs and give praise to God, and that is why the Negro shouts so much in church. But after he was through with the first he got hold of the school book and went from his A B C to Z, and what has happened in fifty years? There is not a white man so educated that you cannot find a Negro to equal him. None in France, none in England, none in America to beat the Negro educationally, and because we stand equal with him we say no longer shall the white man lead us, but we shall lead ourselves.

THE NEGRO AND THE GUN AND POWDER

If we had not a complete training in knowledge before 1914 in that we only knew the book and were only able to read and write, they of themselves gave us training and placed two million of us in the army and gave us gun and powder and taught us how to use them. That completed the education of the Negro. Therefore, tonight the Negro stands complete in education. He knows how to read his book, he knows how to figure out, and he knows how to use the sword and the gun. And because he can do these things so splendidly, he is determined that he shall carve the way for himself to true liberty and democracy which the white man denied him after he was called out to shed his blood on the battlefields of France and Flanders.

THE BLACK STAR LINE STEAMSHIP CORPORATION

I did not come down to Newport News to talk to you merely from a sentimental standpoint. I have come to talk to you from a sentimental and business standpoint. We cannot live on sentiment. We have to live on the material production of the world. I am here representing the Black Star Line Steamship Corporation of the world. The purpose of the Black Star Line Steamship Corporation is to float a line of steamships to run between America, Canada, the Westindies, South and Central America and Africa, carrying freight and passengers, thus linking up the sentiment and wealth of the four hundred million Negroes of the world. Every day I spend away from New York means a financial loss of $5,000 a day; but I have sacrificed all that to come and speak to you in Newport News, because you in Newport News have a history in connection with the Black Star Line.

FIRST STOCK SOLD

I want to say to you that on the 31st of this month the S.S. Frederick Douglass will sail out of New York harbour, the property of the Black Star Line – the property of the Negro peoples of the world. I also want you to understand that the first stock that was sold in the Black Star Line was sold in the Dixie Theatre in Newport News.

(Cheers.) The first five hundred dollars that we sold was sold in Newport News. Therefore, you gave the real start to the Black Star Line, and as you started the Black Star Line we want to finish the Black Star Line.

So that is why I took the chance of leaving New York to speak to you in Newport News. I telegraphed your President a few days ago and asked him up to a conference to let him see what New York is doing to come back and tell you. The Negroes are alive in New York and they are alive in Philadelphia also. New York is supplying its quota to the Black Star Line and so is Philadelphia. I have taken the chance to come to Newport News to find out if you are going to supply your quota towards the Black Star Line. I want you to understand that opportunity is now knocking at your door. You know that opportunity knocks but once at every man's door. The Black Star Line is the biggest industrial and commercial undertaking of the Negro of the Twentieth Century. The Black Star Line opens up the industrial and commercial avenues that were heretofore closed to Negroes.

THE NEGRO MUST PROTECT HIMSELF

Every ship, every house, every store the white man builds, he has his gun and powder to protect them. The white man has surrounded himself with all the protection necessary to protect his property. The Japanese Government protects the yellow man, and the English, German, French and American Governments protect the white man, and the Negro has absolutely no protection. And that is why they lynch and burn us with impunity all over the world, and they will continue to do so until the Negro starts out to protect himself. The Negro cannot protect himself by living alone – he must organize. When you offend one white man in America, you offend ninety millions of white men. When you offend one Negro, the other Negroes are unconcerned because we are not organized. Not until you can offer protection to your race as the white man offers protection to his race, will you be a free and independent people in the world.

Printed in *Negro World,* 1 November 1919

8. The New Negro Has Made History for Himself and Ethiopia Shall Be Redeemed

Fellowmen of the Negro Race,
Greeting: –

The Eternal has happened. For centuries the black man has been taught by his ancient overlords that he was "nothing," is "nothing" and never shall be "anything."

We black folks believe so much in the omnipotence of the white man that we actually gave in all hope and resigned ourselves to the positions of slaves and serfs for nearly five hundred years. But, thank God, a new day has dawned and all black men of the twentieth century see themselves the equal of all men.

Five years ago the Negro Universal was sleeping upon his bale of cotton in the South of America; he was steeped in mud in the banana fields of the Westindies and Central America, seeing no possible way of extricating himself from the environments; he smarted under the lash of the new taskmaster in Africa; but alas! today he is the new man who has proclaimed to the world that the despised and rejected shall rise, not only from his serfdom and slavery, but to rule and to teach man how to live. The New Negro has risen in the might of his manhood and he has now determined within himself to hold fast to the material glories of life and play his part as a man. There is no going back today in the progress of mankind. The white man has been going forward for thousands of years; the yellow man within the last century made a sprint for commercial, industrial, political and scientific glory and he is now regarded as the equal of his white brother on all lines. The Negro who slept and wallowed in the mire for centuries has just begun to turn and he has now placed his hope in God and himself and he is going forward to achieve.

On the 31st of October the Negro people of the world, acting through six thousand of their representatives in New York, United States of America, purchased a steamship which they are re-christening the S.S. Frederick Douglass; and they said: "We are doing this because we desire to get our share of the world's goods, so long as creation lasts." The object was to run a line of steamships between the United States, Africa, Canada, the Westindies and Central America. Thousands of black men and white men said that it could not be done. They said that the Negro had no initiative; that he was not a business man, but a labourer; that he had not the brain to engineer a corporation, to own and run ships; that he had no knowledge of navigation, therefore the proposition was impossible.

"Oh! ye of little faith." The Eternal has happened. The Negro Incorporated, a steamship enterprise by the name of the "Black Star Line;" he placed $500,000 of common stock on the market at $5 a share, and in ten weeks he sold so many shares to his own people that he was able on the 31st of October to take over the first steamship ever owned by the race in modern times. On the 23rd of November the ship sailed out of New York harbour with a Negro captain and Negro crew – a sight that was witnessed by nearly 15,000 people and at the time of writing she is now discharging a load of cement at Sagua, Cuba, in the Westindies.

Verily the Negro had arisen and today he has entered the race of life. He means to play his part and play it well. No more lack of faith, no more lack of confidence, no more belief in the omnipotence of others. The Negro is now a full-grown and wide-awake MAN.

Sons and daughters of Ethiopia, I say unto you, arise! The hour has struck, and Ethiopia is now calling you to achievements and to glory. Let no other sound attract your notice. Heed not the call of any other "voice," for Ethiopia has caught a new vision, and Ethiopia now says, "On to glory."

I beseech you, men and women of the race, to steel you hearts, your minds and your souls for the coming conflict of ideals. The whole world is in turmoil and a revolution threatens. Asia and Europe are preparing for this revolution. It will mean the survival of the fittest, and I now declare that Africa must also prepare; for in the triumph of the forces of white, yellow or black men in this coming revolution will hang the destiny of the world.

Sons and daughters of Africa, scattered though you may be, I implore of you to prepare. Prepare in all ways to strengthen the hands of Mother Africa. Our mother has been bleeding for centuries from the injuries inflicted upon her by a merciless foe. The call is for a physician to heal the wounds, and there can be no other physician than the dark hued son of the mother, and there can be no other nurse as tender and kind as the daughter of this afflicted mother.

Let us not turn back in this determination of ours. Africa must be redeemed, but before her redemption we have to prove to the world that we are fit. The chance to make ourselves fit is now presented to every son and daughter of Africa. We must now achieve in commerce, science, education, art, industry and politics. The Black Star Line Steamship Corporation of 56 West 135th Street, New York, is leading the way for the success of the race in commerce and industry. This corporation desires the assistance of every black man, woman and child. The hope of this corporation is to have the ships of the Negro float on every sea. Our commerce shall extend to every nook and corner of the world, through the Black Star Line; it is therefore up to each and every one of the race to do his and her duty by buying shares in this corporation to make it a powerful agency for good. You may buy your shares today and help to found the empire of greatness for the race. Send in or call right now for your shares. Buy 5, 10, 20, 30, 40, 50, 100 or 200. Get busy, every man, for the Eternal has happened.

The biggest thing for the Negro today is the Black Star Line Steamship Corporation, 56 West 135th Street, New York, United States of America. With very best wishes for your success, yours fraternally,

MARCUS GARVEY

Printed in *Negro World,* 6 December 1919

9. Declaration of Rights of the Negro Peoples of the World

Preamble

Be It Resolved, *That the Negro people of the world, through their chosen representatives in convention assembled in Liberty Hall, in the City of New York and United States of America, from August 1 to August 31, in the year of our Lord, one thousand nine hundred and twenty, protest against the wrongs and injustices they are suffering at the hands of their white brethren, and state what they deem their fair and just rights, as well as the treatment they purpose* [propose?] *to demand of all men in the future.*

We complain:

1. That nowhere in the world, with few exceptions, are black men accorded equal treatment with white men, although in the same situation and circumstances, but, on the contrary, are discriminated against and denied the common rights due to human beings for no other reason than their race and colour.

We are not willingly accepted as guests in the public hotels and inns of the world for no other reason than our race and colour.

2. In certain parts of the United States of America our race is denied the right of public trial accorded to other races when accused of crime, but are lynched and burned by mobs, and such brutal and inhuman treatment is even practiced upon our women.

3. That European nations have parcelled out among them and taken possession of nearly all of the continent of Africa, and the natives are compelled to surrender their lands to aliens and are treated in most instances like slaves.

4. In the southern portion of the United States of America, although citizens under the Federal Constitution, and in some States almost equal to the whites in population and are qualified land owners and taxpayers, we are, nevertheless, denied all voice in the making and administration of the laws and are taxed without representation by the State governments, and at the same time compelled to do military service in defense of the country.

5. On the public conveyances and common carriers in the southern

portion of the United states we are jim-crowed and compelled to accept separate and inferior accommodations, and made to pay the same fare charged for first-class accommodations, and our families are often humiliated and insulted by drunken white men who habitually pass through the jim-crow cars going to the smoking car.

6. The physicians of our race are denied the right to attend their patients while in the public hospitals of the cities and States where they reside in certain parts of the United States.

Our children are forced to attend inferior separate schools for shorter terms than white children, and the public school funds are unequally divided between the white and coloured schools.

7. We are discriminated against and denied an equal chance to earn wages for the support of our families, and in many instances are refused admission into labour unions and nearly everywhere are paid smaller wages than white men.

8. In the Civil Service and departmental offices we are everywhere discriminated against and made to feel that to be a black man in Europe, America and the Westindies is equivalent to being an outcast and a leper among the races of men, no matter what the character attainments of the black men may be.

9. In the British and other Westindian islands and colonies Negroes are secretly and cunningly discriminated against and denied those fuller rights of government to which white citizens are appointed, nominated and elected.

10. That our people in those parts are forced to work for lower wages than the average standard of white men and are kept in conditions repugnant to good civilized tastes and customs.

11. That the many acts of injustices against members of our race before the courts of law in the respective islands and colonies are of such nature as to create disgust and disrespect for the white man's sense of justice.

12. Against all such inhuman, unchristian and uncivilized treatment we here and now emphatically protest, and invoke the condemnation of all mankind.

In order to encourage our race all over the world and to stimulate it to overcome the handicaps and difficulties surrounding it, and to push forward to a higher and grander destiny, we demand and insist on the following Declaration of Rights:

1. Be it known to all men that whereas all men are created equal

and entitled to the rights of life, liberty and the pursuit of happiness, and because of this we, the duly elected representatives of the Negro peoples of the world, invoking the aid of the just and Almighty God, do declare all men, women and children of our blood throughout the world free denizens, and do claim them as free citizens of Africa, the Motherland of all Negroes.

2. That we believe in the supreme authority of our race in all things racial; that all things are created and given to man as a common possession; that there should be an equitable distribution and apportionment of all such things, and in consideration of the fact that as a race we are now deprived of those things that are morally and legally ours, we believed it right that all such things should be acquired and held by whatsoever means possible.

3. That we believe the Negro, like any other race, should be governed by the ethics of civilization, and therefore should not be deprived of any of those rights or privileges common to other human beings.

4. We declare that Negroes, wheresoever they form a community among themselves should be given the right to elect their own representatives to represent them in Legislatures, courts of law, or such institutions as may exercise control over that particular community.

5. We assert that the Negro is entitled to even-handed justice before all courts of law and equity in whatever country he may be found, and when this is denied him on account of his race or colour such denial is an insult to the race as a whole and should be resented by the entire body of Negroes.

6. We declare it unfair and prejudicial to the rights of Negroes in communities where they exist in considerable numbers to be tried by a judge and jury composed entirely of an alien race, but in all such cases members of our race are entitled to representation on the jury.

7. We believe that any law or practice that tends to deprive any African of his land or the privileges of free citizenship within his country is unjust and immoral, and no native should respect any such law or practice.

8. We declare taxation without representation unjust and tyran-[n]ous, and there should be no obligation on the part of the Negro to obey the levy of a tax by any law-making body from which he is excluded and denied representation on account of his race and colour.

9. We believe that any law especially directed against the Negro to his detriment and singling him out because of his race or colour is unfair and immoral, and should not be respected.

10. We believe all men entitled to common human respect and that our race should in no way tolerate any insults that may be interpreted to mean disrespect to our race or colour.

11. We deprecate the use of the term "nigger" as applied to negroes, and demand that the word "Negro" be written with a capital "N."

12. We believe that the Negro should adopt every means to protect himself against barbarous practices inflicted upon him because of colour.

13. We believe in the freedom of Africa for the Negro people of the world, and by the principle of Europe for the Europeans and Asia for the Asiatics, we also demand Africa for the Africans at home and abroad.

14. We believe in the inherent right of the Negro to possess himself of Africa and that his possession of same shall not be regarded as an infringement on any claim or purchase made by any race or nation.

15. We strongly condemn the cupidity of those nations of the world who, by open aggression or secret schemes, have seized the territories and inexhaustible natural wealth of Africa, and we place on record our most solemn determination to reclaim the treasures and possession of the vast continent of our forefathers.

16. We believe all men should live in peace one with the other, but when races and nations provoke the ire of other races and nations by attempting to infringe upon their rights [,] war becomes inevitable, and the attempt in any way to free one's self or protect one's rights or heritage becomes justifiable.

17. Whereas the lynching, by burning, hanging or any other means, of human beings is a barbarous practice and a shame and disgrace to civilization, we therefore declare any country guilty of such atrocities outside the pale of civilization.

18. We protest against the atrocious crime of whipping, flogging and overworking of the native tribes of Africa and Negroes everywhere. These are methods that should be abolished and all means should be taken to prevent a continuance of such brutal practices.

19. We protest against the atrocious practice of shaving the heads of Africans, especially of African women or individuals of Negro blood, when placed in prison as a punishment for crime by an alien race.

20. We protest against segregated districts, separate public con-

veyances, industrial discrimination, lynchings and limitations of political privileges of any Negro citizen in any part of the world on account of race, colour or creed, and will exert our full influence and power against all such.

21. We protest against any punishment inflicted upon a Negro with severity, as against lighter punishment inflicted upon another of an alien race for like offense, as an act of prejudice and injustice, and should be resented by the entire race.

22. We protest against the system of education in any country where Negroes are denied the same privileges and advantages as other races.

23. We declare it inhuman and unfair to boycott Negroes from industries and labour in any part of the world.

24. We believe in the doctrine of the freedom of the press, and we therefore emphatically protest against the suppression of Negro newspapers and periodicals in various parts of the world, and call upon Negroes everywhere to employ all available means to prevent such suppression.

25. We further demand free speech universally for all men.

26. We hereby protest against the publication of scandalous and inflammatory articles by an alien press tending to create racial strife and the exhibition of picture films showing the Negro as a cannibal.

27. We believe in the self-determination of all peoples.

28. We declare for the freedom of religious worship.

29. With the help of Almighty God we declare ourselves the sworn protectors of the honour and virtue of our women and children, and pledge our lives for their protection and defense everywhere and under all circumstances from wrongs and outrages.

30. We demand the right of an unlimited and unprejudiced education for ourselves and our posterity forever[.]

31. We declare that the teaching in any school by alien teachers to our boys and girls, that the alien race is superior to the Negro race, is an insult to the Negro people of the world.

32. Where Negroes form a part of the citizenry of any country, and pass the civil service examination of such country, we declare them entitled to the same consideration as other citizens as to appointments in such civil service.

33. We vigorously protest against the increasingly unfair and unjust

treatment accorded Negro travellers on land and sea by the agents and employees of railroad and steamship companies, and insist that for equal fare we receive equal privileges with other travellers of other races.

34. We declare it unjust for any country, State or nation, to enact laws tending to hinder and obstruct the free immigration of Negroes on account of their race and colour.

35. That the right of the Negro to travel unmolested throughout the world be not abridged by any person or persons, and all Negroes are called upon to give aid to a fellow Negro when thus molested.

36. We declare that all Negroes are entitled to the same right to travel over the world as other men.

37. We hereby demand that the governments of the world recognize our leader and his representatives chosen by the race to look after the welfare or our people under such governments.

38. We demand complete control of our social institutions without interference by any alien race or races.

39. That the colours, Red, Black, and Green, be the colours of the Negro race.

40. Resolved, That the anthem "Ethiopia, Thou Land of Our Fathers etc.," shall be the anthem of the Negro race. (Copy anthem appended.)

The Universal
Ethiopian Anthem
Poem By Burrell and Ford,

I.

Ethiopia, thou land of our fathers,
　　Thou land where the gods loved to be,
As storm cloud at night sudden gathers
　　Our armies come rushing to thee.
We must in the fight be victorious
　　When swords are thrust outward to glean;
For us will the vict'ry be glorious
　　When led by the red, black and green

Chorus

Advance, advance to victory,
Let Africa be free;
Advance to meet the foe
With the might
Of the red, the black and the green.

II.

Ethiopia, the tyrant's falling,
    Who smote thee upon thy knees
And thy children are lustily calling
    From over the distant seas.
Jehovah the Great One has heard us,
    Has noted our sighs and our tears,
With His Spirit of Love he has stirred us
    To be One through the coming years.
    CHORUS – Advance, advance, etc.

III.

O, Jehovah, thou God of the ages
    Grant unto our sons that lead
The wisdom Thou gave to Thy sages
    When Israel was sore in need.
Thy voice thro' the dim past has spoken,
    Ethiopia shall stretch forth her hand,
By Thee shall all fetters be broken
    And Heav'n bless our dear fatherland,
    CHORUS – Advance, advance, etc.

41. We believe that any limited liberty which deprives one of the complete rights and prerogatives of full citizenship is but a modified form of slavery.

42. We declare it an injustice to our people and a serious impediment to the health of the race to deny to competent licensed Negro physicians the right to practice in the public hospitals of the communities in which they reside, for no other reason than their race and colour.

43. We call upon the various government[s] of the world to accept and acknowledge Negro representatives who shall be sent to the

said governments to represent the general welfare of the Negro peoples of the world.

44. We deplore and protest against the practice of confining juvenile prisoners in prisons with adults, and we recommend that such youthful prisoners be taught gainful tracks under human[e] supervision.

45. Be it further resolved, That we as a race of people declare the United Nations null and void as far as the Negro is concerned, in that it seeks to deprive Negroes of their liberty.

46. We demand of all men to do unto us as we would do unto them, in the name of justice; and we cheerfully accord to all men all the rights we claim herein for ourselves.

47. We declare that no Negro shall engage himself in battle for an alien race without first obtaining the consent of the leader of the Negro people of the world, except in a matter of national self-defence.

48. We protest against the practice of drafting Negroes and sending them to war with alien forces without proper training, and demand in all cases that Negro soldiers be given the same training as the aliens.

49. We demand that instructions given Negro children in schools include the subject of "Negro History," to their benefit.

50. We demand a free and unfettered commercial intercourse with all the Negro people of the world.

51. We declare for the absolute freedom of the seas for all peoples.

52. We demand that our duly accredited representatives be given proper recognition in all leagues, conferences, conventions or courts of international arbitration wherever human rights are discussed.

53. We proclaim the 31st day of August of each year to be an international holiday to be observed by all Negroes.

54. We want all men to know that we shall maintain and contend for the freedom and equality of every man, woman and child of our race, with our lives, our fortunes and our sacred honour.

These rights we believe to be justly ours and proper for the protection of the Negro race at large, and because of this belief we, on behalf of the four hundred million Negroes of the world, do pledge herein the sacred blood of the race in defence, and we hereby subscribe our names as a guarantee of the truthfulness and faithfulness hereof, in the presence of Almighty God, on this 13th day of August, in the year of our Lord one thousand nine hundred and twenty.

SIGNATURES:

Marcus Garvey, James D. Brooks, James W.H. Eason, Henrietta Vinton Davis, Lionel Winston Greenidge, A[dr]ian Fitzroy Johnson, Rudolph Ethe[l]bert Brissaac Smith, Charles Augustus Petioni, Rev. Thomas H.N. Simon, Richard Hilton Tobitt, George Alexander McGuire, Rev. Peter Edward Batson, Reynold R Felix, Harry Walters Kirby, Sarah Branch, Mme, Marie Barrier Houston, Mrs Georgie L. O'Brien, F.O. Ogilvie, Arden A. Bryan, Benjamin Dyett, Marie Duchaterlier, John Phillip Hodge, Theophilus H. Saunders, Wilford H. Smith, Gabriel E. Stewart, Arnold Josiah Ford, Lee Crawford, William McCartney, Adina Clem. James, William Musgrave LaMotte, John Sydney de Bourg, Arnold S. Cunning, Vernal J. Williams, Francis Wilcem Ellegor, J. Frederick Selkridge, Innis Abel Horsford, Cyril A. Crichlow, Rev. Samuel McIntyre, Rev. John Thomas Wilkins, Mary Thurston, John G. Befue, William Ware, Rev. J.A. Lewis, O.C. Kelly, Venture R. Hamilton, R.H. Hodge, Edward Alfred Taylor, Ellen Wilson, G.W. Wilson, Richard Edward Riley, Miss Nellie Grant Whiting, G.W. Washington, Maldena Miller, Gertrude Davis, James D. Williams, Emily Christmas Kinch, Dr D.D. Lewis, Nettie Clayton, Partheria Hills, Janie Jenkins, John C. Simons, Alphonso A. Jones, Allen Hobbs, Re[y]nold Fitzgerald Austin, James Benjamin Yearwood, Frank O. Raines, Shedric[k] Williams, John Edward Ivey, Frederick Augustus Toote, Philip Hemmings, Rev. F.F. Smith, D.D. Rev. E.J. Jones, Rev. Dr Joseph Josia Cranston, Frederick Samuel Ricketts, Dugald Augustus Wade, E.E. Nelom, Florida Jenkins, Napoleon J. Francis, Joseph D. Gibson, J.P. Jasper, J.W. Montgomery, David Benjamin, J. Gordon, Harry E. Ford, Carrie M. Ashford, Andrew N. Willis, Lucy Sands, Louise Woodson, George D. Creese, W.A. Wallace, Thomas E. Bagley, James Young, Prince Alfred McConney, John E. Hudson, Wiliam Ines, Harry R. Watkins, C.L. Halton, J.T. Bailey, Ira Joseph Toussa[i]nt Wright, T.H. Golden, Abraham Benjamin Thomas, Richard C. Noble, Walter Green, C.S. Bourne, G.F. Bennett, B.D. Levy. Mrs Mary E. Johnson, Lionel Antonio Francis, Carl Roper, E.R. Donowa, Philip Van Putten, I. Braithwaite, Rev. Jesse W. Luck, Oliver Kaye, J.W. Hudspeth, C.B. Lovell, William C. Matthews, A. Williams, Ratford E.M. Jack, H. Vinton Plummer, Randolph Phillips, A.I. Bailey, duly elected representatives of the Negro people of the world.

Printed in *Negro World*, 11 September 1920.

10. An Exposé of the Caste System Among Negroes

(Written from the Tombs Prison August 31st, 1923)

The policy of the Universal Negro Improvement Association is so clean-cut, and my personal views are so well known, that no one, for even one moment, could reasonably accuse us of having any other desire than that of working for a united Negro race.

The Program of the Universal Negro Improvement Association is that of drawing together, into one universal whole, all the Negro peoples of the world, with prejudice toward none. We desire to have every shade of colour, even those with one drop of African blood, in our fold; because we believe that none of us, as we are, is responsible for our birth; in a word, we have no prejudice against ourselves in race. We believe that every Negro racially is just alike, and, therefore, we have no distinction to make, hence wherever you see the Universal Negro Improvement Association you will find us giving every member of the race an equal chance and opportunity to make good.

Unfortunately, there is a disposition on the part of a certain element of our people in America, the Westindies and Africa, to hold themselves up as the "better class" or "privileged" group on the caste of colour.

This subject is such a delicate one that no-one is honest enough to broach it, yet the evil of it is working great harm to our racial solidarity, and I personally feel it my duty to right now bring it to the attention of all concerned. The Universal Negro Improvement Association is founded on truth, and, therefore, anything that would menace or retard the race must be gotten out of the way, hence our stand in this direction. During the early days of slavery our people were wrested from the bosom of our native land – Africa – and brought into these climes. For centuries, against their will, our mothers were subjected to the most cruel and unfair treatment, the result of which has created among us a diversity of colours and types, to the end that we have become the most mixed race in the world.

THE ABUSE OF OUR RACE

The abuse of our race was, up to eighty-five years ago in the Westindies and fifty-seven years ago in America, beyond our control, because we were then but chatttel slaves of our masters; but since emancipation we have had full control of our own moral-social life and cannot, therefore, complain against anyone other than ourselves, for any social or moral wrongs inflicted upon us.

The Universal Negro Improvement Association realizes that it is now our duty to socially and morally steady ourselves, hence our desire to bring about a united race with one moral code and principle. The types in our race should not be blameable to our generation, but to the abuse and advantage taken of us in the past; but that should not be reason for us to further open ourselves to a continuation of his abuse and thereby wreck our racial pride and self-respect. The Universal Negro Improvement Association believes that the time has come for us to call a halt, and thus steady ourselves on the basis of race and not be allowed to drift along in the world as the outcasts or lepers of society, to be laughed at by every other race beneath their social breath.

NEAR WHITES

Some of us in America, the Westindies and Africa believe that the nearer we approach the white man in colour the greater our social standing and privilege and that we should build up an "aristocracy" based upon caste of colour and not achievement in race. It is well known, although no one is honest enough to admit it, that we have been for the past thirty years at least, but more so now than ever, grading ourselves for social honour and distinction on the basis of colour. That the average success in the race has been regulated by colour and not by ability and merit; that we have been trying to get away from the pride of race into the atmosphere of colour worship, to the damaging extent that the whole world has made us its laughing stock.

There is no doubt that a race that doesn't respect itself forfeits the respect of others, and we are in the moral-social position now of losing the respect of the whole world.

There is a subtle and underhand propaganda fostered by a few men of colour in America, the Westindies and Africa to destroy the self-respect and pride of the Negro race by building up what is commonly known to us as a "blue vein" aristocracy and to foster same as the social and moral standard of the race. The success of this effort is very much marked in the Westindies, and coming into immediate recognition in South Africa, and is now gaining much headway in America under the skilful leadership of the National Association for the Advancement of "Coloured" People and their silent but scattered agents.

The observant members of our race must have noticed within recent years a great hostility between the National Association for the Advancement of "Coloured" people and the Universal "Negro" Improvement Association, and must have wondered why Du Bois writes so bitterly against Garvey and vice versa. Well, the reason is plainly to be seen after the following explanation:

GROUP THAT HATES NEGRO

Du Bois represents a group that hates the Negro blood in its veins, and has been working subtly to build up a caste aristocracy that would socially divide the race into two groups: One the superior because of colour caste, and the other the inferior, hence the pretentious work of the National Association for the Advancement of "Coloured" People. The programme of deception was well arranged and under way for success when Marcus Garvey arrived in America, and he, after understudying the artful doctor and the group he represented, fired a "bomb" into the camp by organizing the Universal "Negro" Improvement Association to cut off the wicked attempt of race deception and distinction, and, in truth, to build up a race united in spirit and ideal, with the honest desire of adjusting itself to its own moral-social pride and national self-respect. When Garvey arrived in America and visited the office of the National Association for the Advancement of "Coloured" people to interview Du Bois, who was regarded as a leader of the Negro people, and who had recently visited the Westindies, he was dumbfounded on approach to the office to find that but for Mr Dill, Du Bois, himself and the office boy, he could not tell whether he was in a white office or that of the National Association for the Advancement of "Coloured" People. The whole staff was either white of very near white, and thus Garvey got his first shock of the advancement hypocrisy. There was no representation of the race there that anyone could recognize. The advancement meant that you had to be as near white as possible, otherwise there was no place for you as stenographer, clerk or attendant in the office of the National Association for the Advancement of "Coloured" People. After a short talk with Du Bois, Garvey became so disgusted with the man and his principles that the thought he never contemplated entered his mind – that of remaining in America to teach Du Bois and his group what real race pride meant.

GARVEY AT N.A.A.C.P.'s OFFICE

When Garvey left the office of the National Association for the Advancement of "Coloured" People, to travel through and study the social life of Negro America, he found that the policy of the Association was well observed in business and professional life, as well as in the drawing room, etc., all over the country. In restaurants, drug stores and offices all over the nation where our people were engaged in business it was discoverable that those employed were the very '"lightest" members of the race – as waitresses, clerks and stenographers. Garvey asked, "What's the matter? Why were not black, brown-skin and mulatto girls employed?" And he was told it was "for the good of the trade." That to have trade it was necessary and incumbent to have "light" faces, as near white as possible. But the shock did not stop there. In New York, Boston, Washington and Detroit, Garvey further discovered the activities of the "Blue Vein Society" and the "Colonial Club." The Westindian "lights" formed the "Colonial Club", and the American "lights" the "Blue Vein" Society. The "Colonial Club" would give annual balls besides regular or monthly *soirées* and no one less than a quadroon would be admitted, and gentlemen below that complexion were only admitted if they were lawyers, doctors or very successful business men with plenty of "cash," who were known to uphold the caste aristocracy. At St Philip's Church, New York, where the very Rev. Dr Daniels held sway and dominion, the "society" had things so arranged that even though this man was a brown-skin clergyman, and his rector a very near white gentleman, he had to draw the line and give the best seats in the church and the places of honour to the "Blue Veins" and the others would have a "look in" when they, by fawning before and "humbling" themselves and by giving lavishly to the church, admitted the superiority of caste. (By the way, Dr Daniels was also an executive officer or director of the National Association for the Advancement of "Coloured" People.) In Washington one or two of the churches did the same thing, but in Detroit the Very Rev. "Bob" Bagnall, now director of branches of the National Association for the Advancement of "Coloured" People held sway. In his church no dark person could have a seat in the front, and, to test the truthfulness of it after being told, Garvey, incog, one Sunday night attempted to occupy one of the empty seats, not so very near the front, and the effort nearly spoiled the whole service, as Brother Bob, who was then ascending the pulpit, nearly lost his "balance" to see such a face so near the "holy of holies." Brother Bob was also an officer of the National

Association for the Advancement of "Coloured" People. On Garvey's return to New York he made (incog) a similar test at St. Philip's Church one Sunday, and the Rev. Daniels was nearly ready to fight.

Now, what does all this mean? It is to relate the hidden programme and motive of the National Association for the Advancement of "Coloured" People and to warn Negro America of not being deceived by a group of men who have as much love for the Negro blood in their veins as the devil has for holy water.

SCHEME TO DESTROY RACE

The National Association for the Advancement of "Coloured" People is a scheme to detroy the Negro Race, and the leaders of it hate Marcus Garvey, because he has discovered them at their game and because the Universal Negro Improvement Association, without any prejudice to colour or caste, is making headway in bringing all the people together for their common good. They hate Garvey because the Universal Negro Improvement Association and the Black Star Line employed every shade of colour in the race, according to ability and merit, and put the N.A.A.C.P. to shame for employing only the "lightest" of the race. They hate Garvey because he forced them to fill Shiladay's place with a Negro. They hate Garvey because they had to employ "black" Pickens to cover up their scheme after Garvey had discovered it; they hate Garvey because they have had to employ brown-skin "Bob" Bagnall to make a showing to the people that they were doing the "right" thing by them; they hate Garvey because he has broken up the "Pink Tea Set"; they hate Garvey because they had been forced to recognize mulatto, brown and black talent in the Association equally with the lighter element; they hate Garvey because he is teaching the unity of race, without colour superiority or prejudice. The gang thought that they would have been able to build up in America a buffer class between whites and Negroes, and thus in another fifty years join with the powerful race and crush the blood of their mothers, as is being done in South Africa and the Westindies.

The imprisonment of Garvey is more than appears on the surface, and the National Association for the Advancement of Coloured People knows it. Du Bois and those who lead the Association are skilful enough to be using the old method of getting the "other fellow" to destroy himself, hence the activities of "brown-skin" Bagnall and "black" Pickens. Walter White, whom we can hardly tell from a Southern gentleman who lives with a white family in Brooklyn, is kept in the background, but dark Bagnall, Pickens and

Du Bois are pushed to the front to make the attack, so that there would be no suspicion of the motive. They are to drive hard and hot, and then the silent influence would bring up the rear, hence the slogan "Garvey must go!" and the vicious attacks in the different magazines by Pickens, Du Bois and Bagnall.

GARVEY CAUGHT THE TUNE

Gentlemen, you are very smart, but Garvey has caught your tune. The conspiracy to destroy the Negro race, is so well organized that the moment anything interferes with their programme there springs up a simultaneous action on the part of the leaders. It will be observed that in the September issue of the *Crisis* is published on the very last page of its news section what purports to be the opinion of a Jamaica paper about Marcus Garvey and his case. The skilful editor of the *Crisis,* Dr Du Bois, reproduces that part of the article that would tend to show the opinion about Garvey in his own country taken from a paper called the *Gleaner,* (edited by one Herbert George de Lisser) and not the property of Negroes.

The article in the original was clipped from the *Gleaner* when it appeared, and was sent by a friend to Garvey, so that he knew all that appeared in it. In it the editor extolled the leadership and virtues of Dr Du Bois, and said it was the right kind of leadership for the American Negro people, and bitterly denounced Garvey. Du Bois published that part that denounced Garvey, but suppressed the part that gave him the right of leadership; and he failed to enlighten his readers that the editor of the *Gleaner* is a very light man, who hates the Negro blood of his mother and who is part of the international scheme to foster the Blue Vein Society scheme. Dr Du Bois failed to further enlighten his readers that he visited Jamaica and was part of the "Colonial Society" scheme; he also failed to state that in the plan De Lisser is to "hold down" the Westindian end of the "caste scheme" and he and others to "hold down" the American end, while their agents "hold down" the South African section.

ENTIRE RACE MUST GET TOGETHER

But now we have reached the point where the entire race must get together and stop these schemers at their game. Whether we are light, yellow, black or what not, there is but one thing for us to do, and that is to get together and build up a race. God made us in His own image and He had some purpose when He thus created us. Then why should we seek to destroy ourselves? If a few Du Boises and De Lissers do not want their progeny to remain of our race, why not be satisfied to abide their time and take their peaceful exit? But why try in this subtle manner to humiliate and destroy our race?

We as a people, have a great future before us. Ethiopia shall once more see the day of her glory, then why destroy the chance and opportunity simply to be someone else?

Let us work and wait patiently, for our day of racial triumph will come. Let us not divide ourselves into castes, but let us all work together for the common good. Let us remember the sorrow of our mothers. Let us not forget that it is our duty to remedy any wrong that has already been done, and not ourselves perpetuate the evil of race destruction. To change our race is no credit. The Anglo-Saxon doesn't want to be a Japanese; the Japanese doesn't want to be a Negro. Then in the name of God and all that is holy, why should we want to be somebody else?

Let the National Association for the Advancement of Coloured People stop its hypocrisy and settle down to real race uplift.

If Dr Du Bois, Johnson, Pickens and Bagnall do not know, let me tell them that they are only being used to weaken the race, so that in another fifty or a hundred years the race can easily be wiped out as a social, economic and political force or "menace."

The people who are directing the affairs of the National Association for the Advancement of "Coloured" People are keen observers, it takes more than ordinary intelligence to penetrate their motive, hence you are now warned.

All the "gas" about anti-lynching and "social equality" will not amount to a row of pins, in fact, it is only a ruse to raise money to capitalize the scheme and hide the real motive. Negroes, "watch your step" and save yourselves from deception and subsequent extermination.

11. First Message to the Negroes of the World from Atlanta Prison

February 10, 1925.

Fellow Men of the Negro Race, Greeting:

I am delighted to inform you, that your humble servant is as happy in sufferng for you and our cause as is possible under the circumstances of being viciously outraged by a group of plotters who have connived to do their worst to humiliate you through me, in the fight for real emancipation and African Redemption.

I do trust that you have given no credence to the vicious lies of white and enemy newspapers and those who have spoken in reference to my surrender. The liars plotted in every way to make it appear that I was not willing to surrender to the court. My attorney advised me that no mandate would have been handed down for ten or fourteen days, as is the custom of the courts, and that would have given me time to keep speaking engagements I had in Detroit, Cincinnati and Cleveland. I hadn't left the city for ten hours when the liars flashed the news that I was a fugitive. That was good news to circulate all over the world to demoralize the millions of Negroes in America, Africa, Asia, the Westindies and Central America, but the idiots ought to know by now that they can't fool all the Negroes at the same time.

I do not want at this time to write anything that would make it difficult for you to meet the opposition of the enemy without my assistance. Suffice it to say that the history of the outrage shall form a splendid chapter in the history of Africa redeemed, when black men will no longer be under the heels of others, but have a civilization and country of their own.

The whole affair is a disgrace, and the whole black world knows it. We shall not forget. Our day may be fifty, a hundred or two hundred years ahead, but let us watch, work and pray, for the civilization of injustice is bound to crumble and bring destruction down upon the heads of the unjust.

The idiots thought that they could humiliate me personally, but in that they are mistaken. The minutes of suffering are counted, and when God and Africa come back and measure out retribution these minutes may multiply by thousands for the sinners. Our Arab and Riffian friends will be ever vigilant, as the rest of Africa and ourselves shall be. Be assured that I planted well the seed of Negro or black nationalism which cannot be destroyed even by the foul play that has been meted out to me.

Continue to pray for me and I shall ever be true to my trust. I want you, the black peoples of the world, to know that W.E.B. Du Bois and that vicious Negro-hating organization known as the Association for the Advancement of "Coloured" People are the greatest enemies the black people have in the world. I have so much to do in the few minutes at my disposal that I cannot write exhaustively on this or any other matter, but be warned against these two enemies. Don't allow them to fool you with fine sounding press releases, speeches and books; they are the vipers who have planned with others the extinction of the "black" race.

My work is just begun, and when the history of my suffering is complete, then future generations of Negroes will have in their hands the guide by which they shall know the "sins" of the twentieth century. I, and I know you, too, believe in time, and we shall wait patiently for two hundred years, if need be, to face our enemies through our posterity.

You will cheer me much if you will now do even more for the organization than when I was among you. Hold up the hands of those who are carrying on. Help them to make good, so that the work may continue to spread from pole to pole.

I am also making a last minute appeal for support to the Black Cross Navigation and Trading Company. Please send in and make your loans so as to enable the directors to successfully carry on the work.

All I have I have given to you. I have sacrificed my home and my loving wife for you. I entrust her to your charge, to protect and defend her in my absence. She is the bravest little woman I know. She has suffered and sacrificed with me for you; therefore, please do not desert her at this dismal hour, when she stands alone. I have left her penniless and helpless to face the world, because I gave you all, but her courage is great, and I know she will hold up for you and me.

After my enemies are satisified, in life or death I shall come back to you to serve even as I have served before. In life I shall be the same; in death I shall be a terror to the foes of Negro liberty. If death has power, then count on me in death to be the real Marcus Garvey I would like to be. If I may come in an earthquake, or a cyclone, or plague, or pestilence, or as God would have me, then be assured that

I shall never desert you and make your enemies triumph over you. Would I not go to hell a million times for you? Would I not like Macbeth's ghost, walk the earth forever for you? Would I not lose the whole world and eternity for you? Would I not cry forever before the footstool of the Lord Omnipotent for you? Would I not die a million deaths for you? Then, why be sad? Cheer up, and be assured that if it takes a million years the sins our enemies shall visit the millionth generation of those that hinder and oppress us.

Remember that I have sworn by you and my God to serve to the end of all time, the wreck of matter and the crash of worlds. The enemies think that I am defeated. Did the Germans defeat the French in 1870? Did Napoleon really conquer Europe? If so, then I am defeated, but I tell you the world shall hear from my principles even two thousand years hence. I am willing to wait on time for my satisfaction and the retribution of my enemies. Observe my enemies and their children and posterity, and one day you shall see retribution settling around them.

If I die in Atlanta my work shall then only begin, but I shall live, in the physical or spiritual to see the day of Africa's glory. When I am dead wrap the mantle of the Red, Black and Green around me, for in the new life I shall rise with God's grace and blessing to lead the millions up the heights of triumph with the colours that you well know. Look for me in the whirlwind or the storm, look for me all around you, for, with God's grace, I shall come and bring with me countless millions of black slaves who have died in America and the Westindies and the millions in Africa to aid you in the fight for Liberty, Freedom and Life.

The civilization of today is gone drunk and crazy with its power and by such it seeks through injustice, fraud and lies to crush the unfortunate. But if I am apparently crushed by the system of influence and misdirected power, my cause shall rise again to plague the conscience of the corrupt. For this I am satisfied, and for you, I repeat, I am glad to suffer and even die. Again, I say, cheer up, for better days are ahead. I shall write the history that will inspire the millions that are coming and leave the posterity of our enemies to reckon with the hosts for the deeds of their fathers.

With God's dearest blessings, I leave you for awhile.

12. Speech at the Century Theatre, London, September 2nd, 1928

THE HON, MARCUS GARVEY (who was received with applause) said: Mr Chairman, ladies and gentlemen – fellow citizens! It was your Shakespeare who said: –

> "There is a tide in the affairs of men,
> Which, taken at the flood, leads on to fortune;
> Omitted, all the voyage of their life
> Is bound in shallows, and in miseries.
> On such a full sea are we now afloat;
> And we must take the current when it serves,
> Or lose our ventures."

Humanity is in the re-making, and every group is interesting itself in that re-making. I represent a group of 400,000,000 Black people who are engaged in this re-making – hundreds of millions of them in Africa, over 100,000,000 of them in India, relics of the African invasion of the earlier centuries; millions of them in South America, descendants of the slaves; other millions in Central America; and millions more in the country now known as the United States of America, and also the Isles of the Westindies, one of which I am from – known as Jamaica.

TALK ABOUT PEACE

We are very much interested in your talk about peace. We are very much interested in your sentimental discussions of the future of the world. Just a few days ago Mr Kellogg; a good old man from the United States of America, journeyed across the Atlantic with a bit of paper; his purpose was to secure signatures to a Pact; the object of it was outlawing war and permanently establishing peace. To the thoughtful mind, to the sober intellect, the whole thing appears so hypocritical and false that I wonder really what is coming to the world. Those of us who have followed the trend of human events within the last half century know well and fully realise how corrupt the world is, especially the statesmanship of the world. A greater era of hypocrisy we have never had than that of the statesmanship of the Twentieth Century. How in the name of goodness intelligent men who claim to be leaders of great groups can imagine that they can, just by signing a bit of paper and making a few statements, put to rest the hopes of millions of down-trodden and oppressed peoples is something marvellous.

EVERYONE WANTS PEACE

Who does not want peace? Everyone wants peace. The black man wants peace – probably more than anyone else, because up to now for the last 3,000 years he has been a man of peace, the proof of which is that today you find him without any battleships or navy, without any standing army, without any big guns, and without any system by which we can take other people's rights or lives. Look around, and wherever you find a black man he is a man of peace. So do not mistake me, that I am for war. I am not. I am out for human justice, and I am sensible enough to know that so long as the robber retains the loot the man who has lost his property cannot be at peace with his vicious neighbour or with anyone else whom he suspects. How, in the name of goodness, do you expect you can have peace in the world when you keep down 400,000,000 Indians, when you keep down 400,000,000 other black people, grind the blood and sweat out of them, kick them from pillar to post? Is it not a farce when you declare for peace without taking these people into consideration?

Who represented the Indians at the signing of this Peace Pact? Not an Indian. Who represented the Africans at the signing of this Peace Pact? Not an African. Yet the lands of these people have been taken away from them; their homes have been ravaged; and those men think they are so smart that they can sign a bit of paper and all those black people will remain quiet for eternity. They are crazy.

REPRESENTING BLACK RACE

I am here representing 400,000,000 black men who are serious – peacably serious; in that we intend to adopt different means to achieve our ends than you have adopted. You have adopted shot and shell – brute force – to attain all that you have accomplished; and when a summary is to be taken and when a judgment is to be passed, Englishmen, I hope you will so act in the Twentieth Century that the crimes of the past will not stand against you. You believe in a God and you say he is to be the final judge of all men. Do you desire your God to judge you by your brute force, by your shot and shell, by your battleships and your dreadnoughts, and by your aeroplanes and the crimes you have committed or by the kindliness of your souls? You taught us about the God that we worship today. We had a different notion of God in the earlier centuries; it was the same being only we worshipped Him through objects we selected; and then you came and you said: "No, you must worship Him in spirit and in truth." We have accepted your philosophy of God; we believe in Him; we believe He is the god of love, of mercy, of justice. We have adopted that fine philosophy of approaching Him and all things human through reason, through judgement, and through brotherly and fatherly love.

That is why I am here this afternoon not as an admiral, not as a general of the army – we could have been – but as a fellow human being appealing to your reason and to your humanity and to your love of God, truth and justice. We 400 million black people desire, late though it be, to restore ourselves to the company of nations, with honour, so that we may show the way to the real peace about which these commercial statesmen are talking today, but do not mean, except, to the extent of more oil monopolies, more diamond monopolies, more rubber concessions, more disarming of the weaker peoples whose lands are so valuable as to supply them, the monopolists, with the resources and wealth that they need.

MR KELLOGG FROM AMERICA

Mr Kellogg came from America to hand in his suggestions about outlawing war. Yet America today is doing – what? America is doing the very thing that foments war. What America would not dare to do to a powerful Empire like Britain, what America would not dare do to a powerful nation like France, what America would not dare do to a powerful nation like Italy – partners in signing this Peace Pact – America, without any reserve, does to Nicaragua and does to Hayti. How preposterous, therefore, for intelligent men to think that there can be any seriousness in discussing peace. One of the principal agents for bringing about peace is doing the very thing that is the principal agency for provoking war. That is not only so of America, it is so of all the Great Powers.

CONDUCT OF EMPIRE

I need not bring to you any information about the conduct of our own empire because as Englishmen you know as much as I do, and probably more than I do. About the attitude of the whole Government towards the subject peoples in Africa and in India. We are not all asleep. It is not because we have not statesmen as able as yours. You have not read our sentiments in your daily papers; and we have not reached the point yet where you will come in daily contact with that sentiment and with that expression; but the future will bring it to you. We want it to come to you without any surprise, and it is because of that why we are endeavouring to prepare you now to realise that the whole world is not so foolish, not so ignorant, and not so much asleep as to think that everything is well and will remain well when in fact the larger number of humanity is struggling, struggling beyond your knowledge, in a terrible state and condition that you would not like even dogs or pigs to be in.

HOWL OF UNEMPLOYMENT

There was a great howl in England about unemployment and about the condition of the poor. If you want to see the poor go to Africa; if you want to see the poor go to India, go to the Westindies and the Southern States of America, where men's souls are driven out by them, where their bodies are harrassed beyond the physical condition of the brute to add to the wealth of the great capitalists who stand behind your statesmen and say: A bigger navy, a bigger army, for the protection of the Empire. But it is not for the protection of the Empire; it is for the purpose of keeping down these unhappy millions in India and Africa and elsewhere so that these few capitalists can continue to grind the last bit of sweat and the last drop of blood out of other human beings. Do you think that that contributes to an order whereby we can all feel happy? Impossible. And I represent this afternoon a large group of unhappy people who have not spoken yet. I lived in America for 14 years, where I was elected as the head of an organisation known as the Universal Negro Improvement Association, which seeks for the higher development of the black race universally. Because I was elected to the position I had to fill it. I had to speak not only my sentiments but the sentiments of the organisation, the sentiments of the people behind the organisation. As I spoke it in America, so I am speaking it here this afternoon. I have personal views of my own – views of fellowship, views of Christian brotherhood with everyone, and I have no enemy in the world. Whether a man be white, yellow, brown or black, if I know nothing about him to the contrary I think of him as a Christian brother and I treat him as such. I therefore do not want you to think that I am expressing my own personal opinion; I am expressing the opinion of 11,000,000 aggrieved negroes, I being only one of the 11 millions. The 11 millions represent 400 millions. When I talk I am not talking for myself, I am talking for those millions of dissatisfied people. These people who are ground down in every part and every section of the world. If you go to the Westindies you will see them; if you go to Central America you will see them struggling under the burden of the day; if you go to South America you will see them smarting under the burden imposed upon them; if you go to East Africa you will see them, outraged by the Colonists; if you go to South Africa you will see them brutalised by a soulless and heartless government under the leadership of Mr Hertzog, a man without a soul where the native is concerned; if you go to West Africa you will see them struggling to free themselves and to be men; if you go to America you will see them lynched and burnt by white mob prejudice and violence. But, under the skilful diplomacy of those who do not desire to see them really free men and whose motives and efforts are directed towards keeping them serfs rather than seeing them develop and becoming a free and independent people as they ought to be, they are being misrepresented.

Those are the people I represent. Those are the people who give me an expression, and so long as these people remain in such a terrible condition as human beings so long will I find cause to go throughout the length and breadth of the world, whether it be in America or in Great Britain or any part of the European Continent, to let humanity know the truth.

SPOKE TRUTH IN AMERICA

I spoke this truth in America for 14 years, as I have said, and all those who were inimical to the interests of negro progress could do was to undermine me and frame me up and imprison me for nearly 2 years and 10 months, thinking that that would be a deterrent not only to my expressions on behalf of the Negroes but that it would be a means of scaring Negroes from continuing the agitation for freedom. Fools that they are, who know not that prison bars cannot deaden or kill the souls and minds of men; fools that they are, who do not realise that there is no power on earth to suppress the hopes of men. They may imprison men by the million, they may execute them by the thousand – as they did to you before you became a free people, as they have done to the Continental nations which have risen through stages of barbarism to what they are; but they shall never stop the machine of progress because that is evolutionary. The black man is in a state similar to yours when you were slaves of another people. You know your history, as Englishmen, too well not to appreciate the stand we take today in working towards the freedom of our country, Africa.

THE HISTORY OF SLAVERY

In a previous speech, at the Albert Hall, I tried to impress you with the history of slavery; how your people took mine from their homes in Africa to the strange lands of the Western world and kept them as slaves for 250 years, kept not only our bodies in slavery but kept our souls in slavery – millions of us. Through the good graces of others of your own race who had more human love and sympathy than your predecessors – notably Victoria of England and Abraham Lincoln of America – we were emancipated and became free men; but even under freedom we are being robbed and exploited and brutalised the world over to an alarming extent and degree.

REASON OF VISIT TO ENGLAND

It is to acquaint you of this that I have been sent to England to speak to you at these public meetings, to speak to you by other approaches, as I have done, to gather your opinion and sentiment touching not only your future but the future of the darker peoples whom you dominate. It is pleasant for me to state that I have some very good responses from some of the most representative men in the country, men with souls; not all of your representatives are heartless, some of your men known in public life sympathise with the conditions of black men in Africa, the Westindies, and America. Those are the men who really save your civilisation; those are the men who really make history better for those of you who have no hearts and those of you who will not think. Because those of you who will not think are equally responsible with those of you who have no heart and act without a heart, because by that action other people are impelled to think unkindly of you, for when you do not instruct your representatives to think and act in the way they should we think unkindly not only of them but also of you. So we are glad there is a softening of feeling when we can find men and women in England who are sympathetic and responsive to the call of others of the human family for help so that they also may enjoy the benefits of the creation which was given to us by God in common. Otherwise your history in contact with other peoples would be a terrible one. Do not you ever make the mistake, Englishmen and women, that you are always going to have the last word in civilisation and in the world. There were other peoples before you. There were black people. Who gave the first civilisation – the black people of Africa. They came before you. Thay had a wonderful civilisation on the banks of the Nile. When the Blue Nile and the White Nile were dotted by universities, by the highest development in art, when Africa right up to Timbuctoo represented the finest culture the world ever saw, your ancestors were living in caves, were living in holes, were savages, were running wild in Continental Europe. The black man passed out of power, giving it to the brown race – the Indians passed it to the Persians and the Chinese, and they in turn, through the same progress of evolution, passed it on to you. The same cycle is going on, and whether you will it or not with your battleships and your dreadnoughts, it will evolve back to another condition. You cannot stop it; it is the force of nature; it is the force of God. You smile and say, "God"; and yet you teach me about God; you say "God" when you believe in science. We believe in Him; and when that God in his prophecy says, "Princes shall come out of Egypt; Ethiopia shall soon stretch out her hands unto God," we do not take it as a mockery nor as a joke, nor that He made a mistake. He placed us here and we are here. We believe in that God – that God has brought us out of slavery without any machine guns.

NEGROES IN AFRICA

Some Colonists interested in Africa had the nerve to tell me the other day that if it were not for the white people the Negroes would have died years ago in East Africa. (Laughter.) Sentimentally the thing would appeal to the man who does not think. But how foolish it is for a man to make such a statement when, without the white man, the Negro lived by himself in Africa and today we have at least 200,000,000 people in Africa. Who preserved them until the white man came? Yet he is telling us that the black people cannot live in East Africa without the white people. That kind of diplomacy is played out and looks foolish to the new thought that permeates the Negro. There is nothing you can tell the black man that he doesn't know. It is true we have to listen to what you say, but it does not mean that we entirely believe it. You are capable of making any statements you like; your statesmen can make them; but it does not follow that we are to accept them. It is true that we have no medium for expressing ourselves; because your Press does not express our feelings and opinions on the matter. It expresses yours. That is why you are in such a peculiar state, because you are hearing only your opinion, one side only – you are knowing only your side; you are not hearing the opinion of the people on the other side and you do not know what they are thinking about.

THINKING ABOUT HUMAN RIGHTS

I am here to tell you what we are thinking about. We are thinking about our rights as human beings, and we are liberal in doing that. We realise that all human beings are entitled to certain rights, and there are no rights peculiar to the white man which we desire to invade. We feel that the white man has certain rights that are natural,that are moral, that are legal, and we would be as ready and as quick to himself to defend him and those rights as he would. If you doubt me, I bring up the history of the war in which we have fought for you. Did you think you could buy us to fight for you in the Nineteenth and the Twentieth Centuries? Do you think you could pay us to fight for you? No, you could not. But when you made your statement and your appeal for help, when you based that statement and the appeal on the larger democracy, and humanity, as Woodrow Wilson did in the last war, the protection of the weaker peoples, that appeal touched our hearts and, without any conscription, without any begging us to help we voluntarily came to your aid in the last war, two millions of us, and we fought like bloodhounds in Mesopotamia, we fought like mad dogs in East Africa. We fought like frenzied men on the various battle fronts in France and Flanders, and we never laid down our arms or rested our heads until we threw the Germans across the Rhine and brought back to you the salvation of your civilisation. We trusted you without asking for reward before we entered, thinking that you were honest and upright in your profession of protecting the rights of weaker peoples. We came out of the war, leaving in Flanders our dead, leaving in Mesopotamia our dead. Then we asked you for consideration, and you said to us in England, "There is no employment for black men; if you happen to be here we will not give you work, but we may give you a little dole for a short while – on which you cannot live – but we will make sure you will get no permanent employment and so after a while you will die, a discouragement for every black man to come to England and the British Isles." You said to us in Continental Europe, "There is no room in Europe for the black man except continually to use him as a soldier in the Rhineland to protect France."

ACCUSED IN GERMANY

When I was accused in Germany of helping to defeat Germany and therefore encouraged the enmity of Germany towards the blacks, I felt ashamed that the German should accuse me of leaving my home in the Westindies and Africa and America to come into Europe to kill him when he did not interfere with me as far as that was concerned. I felt ashamed, and I had to hang my head. But I was doing the best I could to help someone whom I trusted – the Allies. And while the German now hates me because I helped to defeat him, the friend for whom I fought, causing me to offend the Germans, leaves me in the cold, and therefore I am still more friendless; I have two enemies now instead of a friend. Is it not a peculiar state to be in? Englishmen, that is your position. We feel very unpleasant about it, and we do not feel happy having it all pent up in our minds. That is why we want you to know about it – quite inoffensively. I hope you will not take anything I have said this afternoon as an offence. God forbid. The truth should offend no man except the villain and the vagabond. You are all Christian people and cannot be offended by what I have said.

SHOULD A FOREIGN FOE INVADE?

Now, you English people, how would you feel if a foreign race, not like yours, should come in here and take everything you have – take away your Parliament, take away your Westminster Abbey, take away your University of London, your St Paul's, your museums, your art galleries, take away all your great industries, take away your land, take charge of you, take your shoes off your feet, take your good clothes off your backs and give you rags to wear and place heavy loads upon your shoulders by way of everyday labour so that you can work for them? How would you like that? Would you like that? I want an answer from you – would you like that? (Laughter.) I am asking you a question – would you like that? (Renewed laughter,) I am sorry to be embarrassing, but it seems like you would like it. If you would like it, my appeal falls flat because you agree that someone else should do that! But I do not believe that your silence means agreement. You could not agree with a condition like that.

But that is what you are doing to us in Africa. You have come into our homes, deceived us in every way under the guise of Christianity – but do not you ever believe I am not a Christian. I believe in God the Father, God the Son, and God the Holy Ghost; I endorse the Nicene Creed; I believe that Jesus died for me; I believe that God lives for me as for all men; and no condition you can impose on me by deceiving me about Christianity will cause me to doubt Jesus Christ and to doubt God. I shall never hold Christ or God responsible for the commercialisation of Christianity by the heartless men who adopt it as the easiest means of fooling and robbing other people out of their land and country. If I indicted Christianity your Bishops would stand aghast. If I told you the history of the London Missionary Society which is followed by the commercial agent and the soldier, you would really try to ask God for pardon for the things that have been done to the poor, defenceless heathens in the name of Christianity.

RECORD OF CHRISTIANITY AMONG THE BLACKS

Have you ever stopped, Englishmen, to read the record of your Christian penetration of the East and the result of it? I want to set you thinking, you Englishmen and women, because I believe the majority of you are good at heart and you do not know, and that is why you smile complaisantly on things as they happen today. Go to your libraries and read the history of Christianity in the lands of the heathens, and compare those lands today and the condition of the peoples there in the twentieth Centurey with the period prior to the advent of Christianity. Practically every African will tell you today that prior to the advent of Christianity he had his own land, he owned it, he lived on it, but today, because of Christianity, it is not his, it is the Lord's. (Laughter.) What a terrible Lord that is, to adopt such methods to take away the property of other peoples. Now, you know, there is no Lord like that. And because that is the result, some of us have changed our opinions and our desires about Christianity. But I have not changed because I am sensible enough and intelligent enough to know that the Lord never intended that as an attitude of those who profess His faith towards others to be brought within the pale of his Doctrine.

UNIVERSAL SPIRIT OF CHRISTIANITY

I really want to see a universal spirit of Christianity, of brotherly love – when all men would be willing to greet each other in sympathy and love. But today, because of the peculiar statesman-ship that rules the world, there is only thought for a certain type of race and group of people, and without them there is no consideration for the rest of humanity. That is not fair. Yet we have the Pope and we have the Archbishop of Canterbury, the two primary representa-tives of Christianity. How do they think they have impressed us who have learnt to think? How do they think we compare their philosophy with human reason? (A VOICE: They are in the swim.) It is illogical; it is ridiculous. And because they have spoken of themselves and we have not spoken, they think it is all right. Now we have started to speak, and I am only the forerunner of an awakened Africa that shall never go back to sleep.

NOT SPEAKING FOR SELF

Remember, I am not speaking for myself. If I were to speak for myself I believe I would be a preacher; I would be a devout man after the fashion of Jesus Christ. That is how I would like to move about the world, because I have a deep feeling for humanity in my soul. But I cannot be myself just now because I have been elected by 11,000,000 peoples to express their thoughts, and I would be a traitor to my oath of service if I did not speak to you as they command me and as they demand of me. I speak so that you may know the truth. The truth will set you free and set them free. We want an everlasting peace; not an hypocritical peace that a few aged men, who have been trained in the school of commercial graft, think of; their interests are so closely allied with their brothers and fellows in similar pecuniary positions like themselves that they cannot see justice outside of their immediate needs and desires. They do not suffer like common men, therefore they cannot interpret the feelings of common men. When Mr Kellogg comes to represent the American people, really he does not represent the American people, he represents about 500 millionaires in America, of whom he is one. He represents a man like Mr Mellon, one of the richest men in the world with hundreds of millions of dollars to protect; such a man wants peace – he would be a fool if he did not want peace, when there are millions of his own countrymen who cannot find bread for the next day. Those latter are the people who are dissatisfied, and these men who represent these great commercial interests say, "We have to get together, all we who have so much at stake, because these fellows will get unruly, so we must have bigger armies and bigger navies, so when these other fellows want to give vent to their grievances we will let loose these armies and navies for the preservation of the State. But it is not for the preservation of the State but for the protection of these few men with hoarded millions. Left alone we would not require such a tremendous overhead expense for navies and armies, but it is the desire of those who have so much more than they should have; why we have to pay these high rates for armies and navies to keep in subjugation people about whom we do not know anything. I am appealing to you for a larger sympathy. Do not misunderstand me, Englishmen and English-women; I am not a fomenter of trouble; I love humanity too much to advocate any disturbance that would make humanity unhappy. I am the head of a great organisation and know what order is – sometimes I am in the midst of 25,000 people in a convention and, as the head of a strong organisation, I must have order and discipline. Do not interpret anything I say as a suggestion of any kind of disorder among black or white. It is only an effort to present the truth, because it is only by this truth that we can have everlasting and eternal peace. We want you Englishmen and Englishwomen to know that the people of India have souls like you; we want you to know that the people of Africa have souls like you; they have passions like you; they are human beings who must live like you; they must have the same attention like you; they must live in good homes to be able to preserve their bodies in a sanitary state; they must have good food in order to maintain their physical strength; they must have advantages and opportunities so that life can be made pleasant. What is life with eternal misery? – and that is what you, by the power of your Empire, impose upon us – eternal misery. Good God! What a day it will be when black, brown, yellow and white meet before that great Throne which Christian men have taught us about, for you to pass your judgement! Good God, shall we go to another Hell other than the Hell we are in now in India and in Africa? O, God, it would be too much for us to bear!

JUSTICE TO DARKER PEOPLES

I asked your presence at this meeting this afternoon to touch the hearts of Englishmen and women so that those who are innocent and know not what is being done in their name may understand and reach the point where they will use their influence to see that justice is done to the darker peoples of the world.

I have not yet approached your Government and my Government, because you have made me by compulsion a British subject, when by election I would be an African citizen – your Government is my Government – I hope to approach our Government in a short while to lay before them certain facts upon which I am endeavouring to enlighten you. I have not approached them yet because I want to test out your sentiment; because I know the Government will do nothing except it is with your approval. Therefore it is better judgement and good sense to find out how you feel first before going to your Executives who represent you in government, so as to know what will be the future of the blacks of Africa. There is no future for us in the Western world. You Anglo-Saxons who have become the Americans of today across the Atlantic, took us into slavery after it was introduced by the Portuguese under the influence of Pope Nicholas V., and took us to America and kept us there as slaves; though you worked us to death 4,000,000 survived and in 60 years we have grown to 15,000,000; and now in America white statesmanship is devising ways and means by which they can, by economic starvation, starve out the Negroes in 50 years so that they will have no more Negro problem. In the last sixty years they have had enough immigration from the European countries to be able to do without the blacks who have brought America up to where she is today. See how ungrateful a certain branch of your race is, after using us for 250 years as slaves and for 50 years as peons and serfs – now that there is a white population in America sufficiently strong to develop the future of America without the black man, they have evolved a system of economic pressure so that the Negro cannot earn enough money to pay the high cost of living, and it is only a question of 50 or 100 years before voluntarily the Negro, by means of economic starvation, will die out in America and there will be no more Negro problem to confront the white man who wants to make America a white man's country. That is the silent method of men like Kelloggg; men without souls where struggling humanity is concerned; men who think they have the last word in intelligence and can fool everyone.

THE NEGRO A DIPLOMAT

Do not forget that the Negro is the greatest diplomat the world has ever seen. It may be immodest for me to say so, but if it had not been for our diplomacy we should not have survived but should have died like the North American Indian. You are dealing with a people who were the first teachers of diplomacy, because we were the first teachers of civilisation. We have not lost all our virtues, although we have slept on them for a long while; but that does not mean death – we were only resting. Today our intellect is virile and strong; and that is why I say you cannot pull the leg of a half-dead cow with impunity; it may develop into a healthy heifer later if it gets the right kind of pasturage; and although you may look upon the black man as insignificant, you do not know what is in the Negro's mind. Why, we have the same playground for science as any other race. Do you know that we can also be as scientific as any other race? Do you know that there are mysteries hidden in Africa that have not been unearthed for the last 3,000 years because the time has not come yet? You have been digging up some of the things we have done in Africa. You have been to Luxor to dig up Tutankahmen's tomb, and so on. When you find these signs of civilisation you are artful enough to say they "belonged to a different branch of the human race." Yet you have not been skilful enough, when you say that, to prove it. The features of the Pharaohs make them nothing else but black men.

RIGHT TO WRITE HISTORY

You assume a right to write history within the last 500 years, and simply because you have been able to dump so many tons of your history in the world and other people have not said anything by way of complaint, you think your history rests there. But a lot of things your Mr Wells has said we Negroes treat as bunk. Mr H.G. Wells may divert civilisation for the benefit of his Anglo-Saxon group, but that does not make it the fact that the people who laid claims to the civilisation he attributed to others are going to give them up easily. The black man knows his past. It is a past of which he can be nobly proud. That is why I stand before you this afternoon a proud black man, honoured to be a black man, who would be nothing else in God's creation but a black man. (hear, hear.)

NOTHING TO BE ASHAMED OF

I have nothing to be ashamed of. Surely I shall not be ashamed of my God who made me what I am. It is said that the group I represent is looking for social equality. We do not want any social equality except with ourselves; but we look for social freedom from everyone and we will return it to them. But we do not want to take charge of your social life and to embarrass you in your social life if you feel like being among yourselves. We are too proud to embarrass anyone but ourselves. So we want you to understand that the time has come for us both, black and white, to be more serious in our thoughts about each other because some of you white men think we are animals; they have given you pictures to look at to make us look like wild animals; they give you pictures of us with rings through our noses, big mouths, and ugly features, and they say, " That is a black man," so that when a child sees a black man in a subway station he shouts "Mamma, mamma, look, black man!' (*indicating.* (Laughter.) But that is the wrong kind of education; because black men have the future in their making, and when you grow up with wrong notions and ideas you may get yourselves into the state of attempting to deal with black men like brutes instead of like men. As evidence of it, you send out to the Colonies some of your colonial administrators, men whom you have trained in your schools to think that the black man is not to be considered; and when they come out in their khaki uniforms they look as cockish as the Maharajahs of Mysore – (laughter) – and when we approach them they want us to take off our hats and to bow and cringe before them. That kind of attitude is of the past. Black men are not going to cringe before anyone but God. Black men have learnt the value of life, the value of self-respect, like white men. We realise that you are men like ourselves and we are men like you. We intend to give you a man's share, and we demand the same from you. It is a 50/50 proposition. There is nothing in England that we black people want but to see you English people prosper and continue, until God calls you, a happy people within the British Isles; and we want to be left alone in our own country, Africa, to develop as God and we ourselves see best. That is all we are asking for. If we live like that there will not be any trouble.

WHAT WE WANT IN ENGLAND

If we want anything in England we either send over and get it or come over and get it. You come over to us and find out what we want and sell us what we want. If we have no coal, we buy coal from you, and so on; if we have not the materials with which to manufacture cloth, and so on, we get them from you. But what we have got that you have not got, you must buy from us and not steal. What right have you to expect me to come across the street to your home or to your shop and buy mill and butter and ham and bacon and fat and oil and bread, and pay you two sovereigns, whereas if you want cloth and coal you come in my backyard and steal it. Do you know what will happen to you? You will be caught one day. That is what happens to a thief who steals in the dark; and we are only saying to the white people of Europe; Do not be so sentimental as to imagine that the other people are still so blind as not to be able to see that they are being unfairly dealt with. You are very skilful; you adopt peculiar methods when you find native people advanced to the extent that they have representative men who can express the thoughts of the masses; you have a peculiar method of diplomacy whereby you weave certain things around them to frame them up, to get them incriminated in some way, so that you can do something to them and say, "He is a criminal; he has been to prison; he cannot represent you."

You tried that game with me, but it did not work with the Negroes. I went to prison because of the cunning and stealing propensities of low-down politicians who would put Jesus Christ in jail for two votes. I can talk about American politics because I have lived in its midst for 14 years and studied it from A to Z. I can tell you of the damnable methods of American white politicians, the methods they will use to get into office. An American white politician would sell his own family, he would sell the whole State, he would sell the name of Jesus Christ across the ballot box so that he could get into office. Because I represented an honourable, moral movement where I would not pay politicians to keep me at the head, they were able to imprison me; and especially because I was a British subject it made it easier for them to dispose of me. They thought when they imprisoned me that they had finally disposed of me; but, fortunately for me, they have given our movement a momentum of 1,000 per cent., and to day my movement is known in all parts of the world; and though an Englishman may treat my words with levity and think I am a fool, as newspapers like the *Daily Sketch* tried to make out, you will find ten years from now, or 100 years from now, Garvey was not an idle buffoon but was representing the new vision of the Negro who was looking forward to great accomplishments in the future. I bless you, as God would have me bless you, with good will; no enmity or malice, only with a desire for you to know the truth. You have heard the one side from your own men; you must hear the other side from the other people. You must hear India's side, you must hear Africa's side; and fortunately it is my good fortune now to speak for Africa, and I feel that at some other time you will hear from India. Let us have a better understanding to know each other better and I think we will have a better world.

NOT ENGLISHMAN BY RACE

I am going to close in five minutes with this application. I am not an Englishman by race, I am a Britisher by nationality. Just as you are true to your Anglo-Saxon race and type – and you would be unworthy if you were not – so am I true to my African race and African type. Before you became Englishmen you were Anglo-Saxons by race. Before a man is born to a nation he is conceived to a race; so his nationality is only accident whilst his race is positive. I am positively a Negro; there is no mistake about it. Not one drop of anybody else's blood in my veins – if there were, I would try to get rid of it by draining it out as quickly as possible so that I could be a 100 per cent. African as you are 100 per cent. Anglo-Saxon. I respect you for your purity of blood, and you ought to respect me for my purity of blood. God intended us to have different outlooks from the social and political points of view; that is why geographically he suited you for Europe and suited me for Africa.

CONDITIONS IN AMERICA

If you go to America you can hardly tell who is a Negro and who is not; because you have half-white Negroes, three-quarters white Negroes, one-fifth Negroes, one-eighth Negroes, one-tenth Negroes – you have a mixture there, all caused by the advantages you have taken of us by bringing us within the pale of your civilisation. You call us "coloured people." Indeed, we are coloured. The great trouble in America is to find out who is white. That is why the white American wants to get rid of the black man so that it will not be a question of whether the American nation will be a mulatto nation or a black nation. America is no better than France; these two nations have got into trouble and cannot get out of it. You were sensible enough not to bring trouble home to England; that is why you are not interested, that is why you are not here to the number of 10,000 this afternoon. If I were in America I would be addressing 25,000 people, because there it is a real problem; it is a nightmare. Every white man in America goes to bed thinking that on the next day a Negro will be President of the United States of America; and judging by the way the Negroes are running an independent ticket and acting against Hoover, it is likely we shall have a Negro President in America. (Laughter.)

But in case the Negroes are unable to elect a President of their own, I am throwing my support for Alfred Smith. Do you know why I am for Smith against Hoover? It is because Smith is a man from the people; Smith is a man who has sprung from the common people , he knows their wants and their heart beats and their pulse. Hoover has been pampered by the monopolist class; he is himself a millionaire; he can only see American politics and American power from the capitalist point of view. You must have read of the great Rubber Combine in America. Hoover was one of the men responsible for sending me to prison because it was to America's interest, and, not only that, but to the interest of certain American capitalists, to have me imprisoned so that Hoover could back Firestone in Liberia in connection with the rubber lands, land which should have been disposed of to us by agreement with the Liberian Govenment. When Firestone found there was a possibility of a shortage of rubber in America and there was nowhere where America could obtain rubber other than from England, they sent their commercial investigators all over the world and they found that it was possible for rubber to be grown in Liberia. Then Hoover backed up Firestone to get the President of Liberia to give up the contract he had entered into with me so that the American Negroes could repatriate themselves and help build up Liberia – to have a permanent and peaceful home of their own – Hoover used his power as Secretary of Commerce not only to imprison me but to take away from the Negroes, a concession that had been given to them and to give it to Firestone so that the natives of Liberia could be exploited for the benefit of American capital. Two years after Firestone went there he reduced the natives to virtual slavery; he got the Government to use the natives to build roads to give access to his plantations; they had to work without proper provision for food and without any pay. Hoover represents in American life people who will do that.

Through my organisation it is my duty, before God and before man, to see to it that a man like that, if possible, is not returned as President of the United States, such a great country with such a great power that can do so much good or ill. That is why I am for Smith, a man who would not tolerate such a method in politics; a man who has been fair and square in all his dealings as Governor of New York State. The Negroes of America can put their trust in him, and I hope he will be returned as President of the United States of America at the next Election.

In conclusion, God bless you Englishmen and women. I trust that you will not take offence at anything I have said today. What I have said has been said so that you may adopt a policy and attitude to us Negroes beyond what is being done to them today. I thank you, and God bless you. (Loud applause.)

Other titles by
Hansib Publishing

INDIA IN THE CARIBBEAN
Ed Dr David Dabydeen and
Dr Brinsley Samaroo
ISBN: 1 870518 00 4 PB   PRICE: £8.95
ISBN: 1 870518 05 5 HB   PRICE: £11.95

INDO-WESTINDIAN CRICKET
By Professor Frank Birbalsingh and
Clem Shiwcharan
ISBN: 1 870518 20 9 HB   PRICE: £7.95

THE SECOND SHIPWRECK:
INDO-CARIBBEAN LITERATURE
By Dr Jeremy Poynting
ISBN: 1 870518 15 2 PB   PRICE: £6.95

THE WEB OF TRADITION:
USES OF ALLUSION IN
V.S. NAIPAUL'S FICTION
By Dr John Thieme
ISBN: 1 870518 30 6 PB   PRICE: £6.95

BENEVOLENT NEUTRALITY:
INDIAN GOVERNMENT POLICY AND
LABOUR MIGRATION TO
BRITISH GUIANA 1854-1884
by Dr Basdeo Mangru
ISBN: 1 870518 10 1 HB   PRICE: £12.95

THE OPEN PRISON
By Angus Richmond
ISBN: 1 870518 25 X PB   PRICE: £4.95

COOLIE ODYSSEY
By Dr David Dabydeen
ISBN: 1 870518 01 2 PB   PRICE: £3.95

A READER'S GUIDE TO WESTINDIAN
AND BLACK BRITISH LITERATURE
By Dr David Dabydeen and
Dr Nana Wilson Tagoe
ISBN: 1 870518 35 7 PB   PRICE: £6.95

ESSAYS ON RACE, CULTURE
AND ENGLISH SOCIETY
By Dr Paul Rich
ISBN: 1 870518 40 3 PB   PRICE: £6.95

100 GREAT WESTINDIAN
TEST CRICKETERS
By Bridgette Lawrence and Reg Scarlett
ISBN: 1 870518 65 9 HB   PRICE: £10.95

BARRISTER FOR THE DEFENCE
By Rudy Narayan
ISBN: 09506664 2 4 PB   PRICE: £6.95

BOOK OF COMMONSENSE
Compiled by Neil Prendergast
PB   PRICE: £6.95

FROM WHERE I STAND
By Roy Sawh
ISBN: 0 9956664 9 1 PB   PRICE: £5.95

MY THOUGHTS, 2nd EDITION
By Pamela Ali
ISBN: 1 870518 06 3 PB   PRICE: £3.95

HOGARTH, WALPOLE AND
COMMERCIAL BRITAIN
By Dr David Dabydeen
ISBN: 1 870518 45 4 HB   PRICE: £15.95

THE CARIBBEAN: GUYANA,
TRINIDAD & TOBAGO,
BARBADOS, JAMAICA
By Steve Garner
ISBN: 1 870518 55 1 PB   PRICE: £6.95

GREAT FIGURES FROM THE
THIRD WORLD
By Liz Mackie and Steve Garner
ISBN: 1 870518 60 8 HB   PRICE: £11.95

SPEECHES BY ERROL BARROW
Edited by Yussuff Haniff
ISBN: 1 870518 70 5 HB   PRICE: £10.95

THIRD WORLD IMPACT
7th EDITION
Edited by Arif Ali
ISBN: 0 9506664 8 3 PB   PRICE: £9.95
ISBN: 0 9506664 8 3 HB   PRICE: £13.95

RASTA AND RESISTANCE
FROM MARCUS GARVEY TO
WALTER RODNEY
By Dr Horace Campbell
ISBN: 0 95066 645 5 PB   PRICE: £6.95
ISBN: 0 95066 645 5 HB   PRICE: £9.95